IMAGES
of America

WEYAUWEGA

MAP OF WEYAUWEGA. Weyauwega is not a large town. Laid out in a grid, the early portion of town was only a small part of present-day Weyauwega. However, it was booming with many stores and businesses. This artist's rendering is from 1870. (Courtesy of the Weyauwega Public Library.)

ON THE COVER: WEYAUWEGA GREETINGS AT THE TRAIN DEPOT. Pictured is the second train depot in Weyauwega, which replaced the first depot after it was destroyed by fire. With rail a mainstay in travel at the time, this was the sight that greeted most visitors to Weyauwega. (Courtesy of Keith Wall.)

IMAGES
of America

WEYAUWEGA

Kim J. Heltemes, Mary Werth,
and Janis Dahlke

ARCADIA
PUBLISHING

Copyright © 2013 by Kim J. Heltemes, Mary Werth, and Janis Dahlke
ISBN 9781531668754

Published by Arcadia Publishing
Charleston, South Carolina

Library of Congress Control Number: 2013939804

For all general information, please contact Arcadia Publishing:
Telephone 843-853-2070
Fax 843-853-0044
E-mail sales@arcadiapublishing.com
For customer service and orders:
Toll-Free 1-888-313-2665

Visit us on the Internet at www.arcadiapublishing.com

AERIAL VIEW. In this c. 1940 aerial view of Weyauwega, note that, when compared to the map on the previous page, things have not changed much in 70 years. The Catholic church can clearly be seen on the right. The wide street that runs center-left to downtown is Main Street. The grain silo on the far right is all that is left of the old rye mill. The fairgrounds on the east edge of town are not pictured. (Courtesy of the Weyauwega Public Library.)

CONTENTS

Acknowledgments   6

Introduction   7

1.   The Beginning, the Mill, and the Square   9

2.   The People   19

3.   Businesses   53

4.   Military   71

5.   Schools and Churches   87

6.   Homes of Weyauwega   101

7.   Downtown   107

8.   Village Life   115

Acknowledgments

A lot of people from Weyauwega stepped forward to help with this project; most of them are the elders of the community. The cover photograph came from Keith Wall, an interesting fellow who has seen more than most and can remember it like yesterday. Ossie Prillwitz and his wife, Gloria, along with Florence Oehlke, were there to help whenever we needed them. Ethel Doede, Ray Hutchinson, and Ann Hutchinson Van Ess were also reliable sources.

The notes saved from Frank Haffner were extremely useful. Librarian Anita Romon had cataloged and organized so much of the community's history that what she saved for us was easy to utilize. The library archives were our backup source. John Ware's *A Standard History of Waupaca County, Wisconsin*, and Wakefield's book of early history were valuable sources.

Others who gave information or photographs were Sherry Brownlow, Mary Van Epps Schultz, Beata and Jon Peterson, Joanne Gettendorf, Steve Liebe, Jeff Pockat, Carol Leupold Toepke, and Jim Waid.

Doing this book would not have been possible without the library trustees and the director, Kristy Pennebecker. Sharon Koenigs was always there for us. The authors would like to thank everyone involved with this project dealing with such old history and materials. We could not have done this alone.

Newspaper editors of years ago wrote much of the history of Weyauwega. Editors like William Tompkins should be given credit for telling the story of the beginning of the town. For Weyauwega's bicentennial, a scrapbook was made, which proved to be extremely useful for information. As an extended version of this scrapbook, a book was compiled that further told the family stories of Weyauwegians. William and Joan Mallo and Mary Werth did *Weyauwega Remembers* as a project of the sesquicentennial. We want the reader to know that this Images of America series book complements that book.

As the book neared its finish, the library celebrated its 100th anniversary. This book is dedicated to the years of the library's existence, the history saved through the library, and to the people, like Anita Romon, who made it possible.

INTRODUCTION

From a Native American interpretation, Weyauwega is said to translate to "here we rest." This little town is located in eastern-middle Wisconsin in an area that was and still is popular with the Menominee Tribe. In 1852, the Menominee signed a treaty that opened Wisconsin to settlement, but people had come into this part of Wisconsin before then. With a river system that comes from Green Bay on Lake Michigan and fur trade companies like the Hudson Fur Trade Company, settlement was bound to happen. The fur trade companies of the French and English brought settlers to a prime hunting and trapping area where waterways were the mode of transportation. The Wolf River took those settlers to what became "Gills Landing," a spot on the Wolf River some 3.5 miles east of Weyauwega. A Mr. Bass built a small inn in Weyauwega for travelers who came from Stevens Point, Wisconsin. The first steamboat, the *Blackhawk*, arrived there in 1843.

The first credited settlers were Henry Tourtellotte, Amos Dodge, and Murray Lewis, who came in 1848. Many had gone through, but these men stayed. A waterway (the Waupaca River) would be ideal to start a sawmill and a gristmill. But a few miles south Evan Townsend, Frank Powers, and a Mr. Lincoln built a sawmill on the Little Wolf River in an area known as Evanswood. Timber was sawn and taken from there to the Weyauwega Main Street area to start businesses and housing. Walter Weed and Benjamin Birdsall located here in 1849 and built a sawmill on the village site. Another important settler, Peter Meiklejohn, came to Weyauwega in the same year.

In 1850 the rush began. Robert Baxter built the first hotel, the American House, and Charles Gumaer opened the first store in Waupaca County. Jacob and Walter Weed, with Benjamin Birdsall, dammed the river to start a flour mill. The man considered to be the one of the founding fathers of Weyauwega, Louis Bostedo, became a partner in the mill.

By 1851 Ira Sumner, hired by the mill, and the Mumbrue family, started to survey and to plot out the village. The Mumbrues had surveyed from Poy Sippi, some 16 miles south, to Waupaca, six miles northwest. They dropped off members of the family along this line to become prime settlers. People like A.V. Balch, the Billingtons, the VanOstranders, Tibbetts, Jennys, and Judge Beals arrived. The Tibbetts built the second hotel, the Weyauwega House. The Post family members set up their first store on an area they cleared away on what became Main Street. The first school was established with Burt Brett as the first teacher. He taught from 1851 to 1853. James Devens also arrived in town.

By 1852, Weyauwega started to take shape. The treaty was signed that opened the land to settlement. Land claims were filed. The Methodist church was organized. And another important person, Andrew Van Epps, arrived. A third hotel, the LaDow House, was built while the first town hall meeting was held at the American House. The Presbyterian church was also organized in 1852, but its place of worship was not built until 1854, when Debius Hutchinson constructed it. An apple tree was planted, and Robert Baxter, attorney John Fordyce, and Louis Bostedo took up permanent residence.

Since the land was opened to settlement, 1853 became the first year that the village plots could be recorded at the land office in Menasha, Wisconsin. An all-important plank road was completed from Gills Landing to town.

The first jail in the county was built in the village in 1854. It was the year Mr. Myers started a 34-mile route of stagecoach service from Gills Landing to Plover. Another church, the Baptist church, was organized, and the village school was started.

In 1855 an important business, the Weed and Gumaer Manufacturing Company rye flour mill, was established. William C. Tompkins started the *Weyauwegian* in July. Charles M. Fenelon and W.A. Weisbrod came to Weyauwega. The Baptist church was built, and Jacob Conrad established the first brewery. By 1855, there were three dry goods stores, a drugstore, a hardware store, four grocery stores, and a cabinet and furniture store.

1856 was the year that really put Weyauwega on the map. It was incorporated as the Village of Weyauwega. The pioneer block was built on the busy corner of Mill and Main Streets. The Masonic building was constructed and was chartered in 1857. By then, there were five churches, one grade school, seven dry goods stores, four grocery stores, three drugstores, two jewelry stores, three hardware stores, two millinery stores, two furniture stores, two shoe stores, one harness shop, one tailor store, two meat markets, four blacksmith shops, a wagon shop, a livery stable, two hotels, two lawyers, two physicians, a newspaper and printing office, a bank, a sawmill, and a gristmill. There also was a basket factory, four saloons, and one brewery, with a population of 650 people.

In 1857, the historic store of the Post brothers, Lorenzo and Joseph, began on Main Street. George W. Taggart became a resident. Weyauwega suffered its first fire of importance at the newspaper office of the *Weyauwegian*. In 1859, A.V. Balch started an insurance company. Charles A. Rice arrived in town. And then, the Civil War took men away in 1861.

William Bauer started his furniture store in 1866. Bank clerk Thomas Wilson settled in 1868. The newspaper, the *Times*, was begun in 1870 by F.W. Sackett, while Weed and Gumaer started a bank in their names. The all-important mode of modern transportation of the time, the train, completed a line from Neenah to Weyauwega in 1871.

St. Peter Evangelical Lutheran Church was organized in 1872 and was built in 1873. It would be the first St. Peter church. A few years later in 1874, H.W. Potter started his general merchandise store, and J.S. Walbridge began his medical practice. A year later, the first county fair was held in Weyauwega. J.C. Keeney started the *Chronicle* in 1877. Dr. J.F. Corbett began his medical practice in 1880.

The blacksmith was an important person in any town on the Western frontier. In 1881, the Kosanke brothers began a blacksmith shop and a hardware store. A.L. Hutchinson was also well known and became the postmaster in 1882; family members still live in town today.

Even though there seemed to have been a lot of activity to this point, the town really took off in 1884. By then, settlers had made their way during a great influx of immigrants. These men were the business owners, the leaders in society. The Grand Army of the Republic Andrew Chambers Post No. 180 was started. W.W. Crane bought out the building and stock of Potter and Company. The center of activity in town was built on the town square, the Whitney Hall. Gebauers Opera Hall was opened to drinking and roller-skating. Another doctor began his practice, the ever popular E.H. Jones.

This gives the reader an idea of what it took to carve a small town out of the wilderness.

One

THE BEGINNING,
THE MILL, AND
THE SQUARE

ACROSS FROM GILLS LANDING. In 1843, to accommodate boat passengers and freight, John Gill established Gills Landing. Several Civil War regiments used Gills Landing when they were sent off to war. Before the railroad in 1871, practically all people and freight came to Gills Landing, the "port of entry" for settlers heading West. Gill had several buildings on site, including a boardinghouse, tannery, and barns. A plank road was built to Weyauwega in 1852. In 1854, Myers began his stage service from Gills to Plover. Herman Steinberg owned a hotel here, but it burned in November 1872. J.A. Vincent, a member of Company B of the 14th Wisconsin Infantry, wounded in the battle of Shiloh, worked at Gills Landing for four years and then engaged in farming. (Courtesy of Kim J. Heltemes.)

GILLS LANDING. John Gill paid $100 while Weed and Birdsall paid $200 for the plank road. Other settlers paid the rest. The road was started in 1852 and was completed in 1853. People picnicked while waiting for paddleboats such as the *Paul L.* Travelers had a choice of boat or train. Eventually, the trains won out. The first train across in 1871 was named *Weyauwega.* (Courtesy of the Weyauwega Public Library.)

HANNAH HOTEL. George Hockstock built the hotel at Gills Landing in about 1900 on the north bank of the Waupaca River, where it flows into the Wolf River. In 1902, the Wisconsin Central Railroad built a depot at Gills Landing. Hockstock was the depot agent and postmaster. Around 1918, Hockstock sold the hotel to Hannah Mortinson of Chicago. (Courtesy of the Weyauwega Public Library.)

THE MILL. This is where the actual settlement of Weyauwega began. In 1848, Amos Dodge, Joseph Hicks, Murray Lewis, and Henry Tourtelotte purchased the water rights of the river and lake here. They began construction of a dam and sawmill. The sawmill was completed in 1850, two years before Indian title to the land expired. One of the first buildings here was a boardinghouse for millworkers. Joseph and Jacob Weed and Benjamin Birdsall finished the dam. In 1855–1856, a flour mill was constructed here, the largest rye mill in the world. (Courtesy of the Weyauwega Public Library.)

WOOD MILL, 1900. This 1900 view of the wood mill shows sawdust piled at the rear of the building. It was alongside the river so that water could be used to drive the saw blades. It must be remembered that these mills along the riverbanks are what got the country built. They made possible the change from log cabins to frame houses, and Weyauwega had its share of fine frame homes. (Courtesy of the Weyauwega Public Library.)

OLD RYE MILL AND DAM. The rye mill was built at a cost of $20,000. The elevator was circular with 20 bins around an open court and had a holding capacity of 40,000 bushels. The mill was driven by waterpower and had five runs of stone and three sets of Gray patent noiseless rolls following a complete overhauling in 1883. The wooden fish ladder can be seen from the bridge. (Courtesy of the Weyauwega Public Library.)

RYE MILL. The mill is shown with the millpond in the foreground. In 1895, Weed and Gumaer Manufacturing Company and Warren Hinchey, plant superintendent, put in an electric light plant and powerhouse at the south end of the dam on the site of the old Henry Steinberg paper mill. The paper mill manufactured wrapping and printing paper. The rye mill closed in 1935. In 1938, a soybean company took it over. (Courtesy of the Weyauwega Public Library.)

MILL FISH DAM. On the backside of the rye mill was the fish ladder/dam on the millpond. The large warehouse was a potato storage building with the Soo Line tracks running alongside. In 1932, Weyauwega Milling Company constructed a concrete grain storage elevator 87 feet high. George Moody was the resident manager of Weyauwega Milling Company when the mill put out 150 bushels of rye flour per day. (Courtesy of the Weyauwega Public Library.)

13

VIEW FROM ACROSS THE POND. In 1904, C.E. Northrup of Waterbury, Connecticut, announced that he would manufacture drills or burrs used by dentists in preparing teeth for filling. Northrup's associates were Warren Hinchey and F.E. Phillips. The plant location was part of the electric light building. Hinchey (1848–1912) was born in New York and died at the age of 64 of influenza. He is buried at Oakwood Cemetery in lot No. 418. (Courtesy of the Weyauwega Public Library.)

THE POWERHOUSE. The powerhouse's interior at the mill shows two unidentified people at the controls. The electric company had a contract with the village for 12 area streetlights. An electric telephone connected the bank with the mill. An additional waterwheel was needed to provide the necessary power to run the electric company. (Courtesy of Kim J. Heltemes.)

WILLIAM BAUER HOME. This is South Mill Street; the white fence is bordering the William Bauer property. It was purchased from Louis Bostedo in 1881. The square, on which the Soldiers Monument was situated, was the town center from the earliest days. The Bauer home is near the northeast corner of the image. There was a park on the southeast corner and Whitney's on the southwest corner. The northwest corner had tennis courts. Two blocks to the north was the business section on Main Street. Louis Bostedo donated the land for the square. The park had a bandstand. The square was on the four corners of South Mill and Sumner Streets. The Soldiers Monument is still on the square but now off the roadway. (Courtesy of the Weyauwega Public Library.)

WHITNEY HALL INTERIOR. Whitney Hall was 40 by 80 feet. This is a shot of the interior with people roller-skating. Roller-skating became popular in the mid-1880s. By December 1884, enough money had been raised by private subscription to build the hall. Besides roller-skating, the hall was used for basketball and community affairs. The date of the photograph is unknown. (Courtesy of the Weyauwega Public Library.)

WHITNEY HALL. This real-photo postcard shows Whitney Hall, but is labeled as the opera house. Whitney Hall burned down in 1919. School graduations, plays, meetings, and dances were held there. The high school's second commencement was held here on June 25, 1890. The people are unidentified. (Courtesy of the Weyauwega Public Library.)

16

CITY PARK. This is the City Park before the Soldiers Monument was moved after vehicles hit it at least three times. The Soldiers Monument was moved from the first location, which was in the middle of the road, to the lawn of the northeast corner of the village square, the present-day clinic's location. Midweek band concerts were held during the summer at the town square bandstand until the 1940s. (Courtesy of the Weyauwega Public Library.)

MILL STREET LOOKING NORTH. Whitney Hall can be seen on the left side of the photograph. The Soldiers Monument is shown in the middle of Mill and Sumner Streets. Note the cement sidewalks on the east side of Mill Street. The Jacob Weed house is on the right with the fence. (Courtesy of the Weyauwega Public Library.)

WEYAUWEGA JAIL. This was the first jail in Waupaca County. It was built in 1854 and was one of the landmarks of the village. After it was one month old, the teacher and students moved to this building with desks and a board fastened against a side wall. The first school was held in a different shanty in 1851 with Mary (Chandler) Dewey teaching. It became a jail after the new Pioneer School opened. (Courtesy of the Weyauwega Public Library.)

WEYAUWEGA PUBLIC LIBRARY. The Weyauwega Public Library was organized in 1912 and first housed in the Exchange Building on the northwest corner of Main and Mill Streets. The village hall on Main Street was built in 1915. At that time, the library was moved to the second floor of the village hall, where it occupied two rooms. A new library was constructed in 1985. Early photographs of the interior are hard to come by. The library recently celebrated its 100th anniversary. (Courtesy of the Weyauwega Public Library.)

Two

THE PEOPLE

LOUIS BOSTEDO. Louis Bostedo (1798–1877) was born in New Jersey. In 1850, Bostedo, shown here around 1865, became a partner in the dam and mill. Bostedo was the first worshipful master of the Weyauwega Masonic Lodge. In 1856, Bostedo was the first village president and was elected to the Wisconsin State Assembly in 1855. His opponents charged falsely that he was a "foreigner . . . only in the country for one year." In fact, Bostedo's ancestors fought in the American Revolution and the War of 1812. He is buried in Oakwood Cemetery. (Courtesy of the Weyauwega Public Library.)

WILLIAM G. GUMAER. William Gumaer was born in New York, on July 26, 1818. He traveled to Vinland, Wisconsin. In 1848, Gumaer formed a partnership with Jacob Weed. Their firm Weed, Gumaer & Co. established the Bank of Weyauwega in 1870. Gumaer was an Odd Fellow in Washington Lodge No. 6 and a Free and Accepted Mason as the first junior warden in Weyauwega Lodge No. 82. He is buried in Oakwood Cemetery. (Courtesy of the Weyauwega Public Library.)

MR. AND MRS. ALBIJAH BENNETT. Albijah Bennett was born in 1836 in Massachusetts. A carpenter and contractor, in 1856 he joined his family in nearby Royalton. In 1859, he traveled on foot to visit his mother in Massachusetts. In 1864, he married Maryetta (Lilley), born in 1839. Albijah, who became a furniture maker and undertaker, retired in 1913. His grandfather Thomas Bennett served in the Revolutionary War. Albijah and Maryetta are shown in their later years. (Courtesy of the Weyauwega Public Library.)

WALTER H. WEED. Walter
H. Weed was the brother of
Jacob Weed. Together with
Jacob and Benjamin Birdsall,
Walter purchased the partial
dam at Weyauwega in 1850.
The partners finished the
dam and built a flour mill
known as Weed, Birdsall
& Co. He opened the
first store in Weyauwega
with Charles L. Gumaer.
He is buried in Oakwood
Cemetery. (Courtesy of the
Weyauwega Public Library.)

GEORGE W. TAGGART SR. George
W. Taggart Sr. (1813–1900) was born
in New York and settled in Lind,
Wisconsin, in 1849. He was the
postmaster in Lind, a teacher, the
first county surveyor, county sheriff,
and a member of the Masonic lodge.
Taggart married Eunice Fulton in
1837, and they had four children. His
son Robert said, "When father came
here, the Indians were thicker than
the automobiles are today—and they
were not half as dangerous." (Courtesy
of the Weyauwega Public Library.)

Lorenzo L. Post. Lorenzo L. Post was born in 1821 in Vermont. He arrived in Weyauwega in 1851 and served as justice of the peace and town chairman. He was a member of the Wisconsin State Assembly in 1878 and 1879. His wife was Elizabeth Simmons. They had two children, Lorenzo D., a druggist with his father, and a daughter, Ella. They lost four other children. (Courtesy of the Weyauwega Public Library.)

Elijah W. Wrightman and A.W. Potter. Elijah W. Wrightman (1820–1892) was another early settler. Elijah (left) and A.W. Potter (right) were inspectors of the first elections of April 1852, held in the home of Robert Baxter. Baxter's home was the American House, a hotel. James Baxter may have been the brother of Robert Baxter. These photographs came from the Masonic photograph album, as both were Masons. Elijah died of heart disease. (Courtesy of the Weyauwega Public Library.)

JAMES E. DEVENS AND HIS WIFE, MARY ANN. J.E. Devens is another of the 1851 settlers. Devens, as a clerk in the Charles L. Gumaer Store with William G. Gumaer, later worked with the Corps of Engineers as they sectioned out the township. Devens married Mary Ann Chambers in 1865, and they had three children. He served as deputy sheriff, sheriff, justice of the peace, and insurance agent. He became a Mason in 1865. This is his Masonic photograph. (Courtesy of the Weyauwega Public Library.)

PETER MEIKLEJOHN. Peter Meiklejohn, born in 1818 in New York, came to Weyauwega in 1849 as one of the first settlers. In 1850, sermons by Reverend Baxter were heard in his Little Wolf River home. In 1851, he was elected county supervisor. He married Hannah Wright, and they had 10 children. Peter served with three men as applicants for incorporation of the Village of Weyauwega. He sold pottery that he manufactured from Weyauwega clay. Meiklejohn, a master Mason, was a member of First Baptist Church. (Courtesy of the Weyauwega Public Library.)

LORENZO "RENO" D. POST. Reno Post was a son of Lorenzo L. Post. He worked in his father's drugstore as the druggist. (Courtesy of the Weyauwega Public Library.)

THOMAS F. WILSON. Thomas F. Wilson, a banker, was born in 1855 in New York City. His father, a tailor, moved the family to Weyauwega in 1868. Thomas Wilson clerked at the L.L. Post Drugstore until 1880, cashiered at the Weed, Gumaer & Co. bank until 1910, and at the Farmers & Merchants Bank. He served as the secretary and treasurer of Hinchey and Phillips Dental Burr Company. Thomas Wilson attended the Baptist church. He was a Mason and village treasurer. This photograph is from the Weyauwega Masonic album. (Courtesy of the Weyauwega Public Library.)

FLORENCE BALDWIN. Florence Baldwin's father, Calvin B., started the Baldwin Creamery. Florence attended school in Evanston, Illinois. She also attended Carroll College in Waukesha, Wisconsin. As a musician, she taught music and played at various events in Weyauwega. Florence married Alvin Thomas. (Courtesy of the Weyauwega Public Library.)

CAROLINE FORDYCE. Shown is the wife of attorney John Fordyce, who settled in Weyauwega in 1852. John was the village president in 1878 and school board clerk in 1879. It is said that they owned the best dairy farm around Weyauwega. He was also a member of the Old Settlers Society, started in 1872 at the Tarbell House. Members had to be in the county for 17 years to join. (Courtesy of the Weyauwega Public Library.)

RENA BAUER. Rena Bauer (1879–1968) was the daughter of William Bauer and the sister of Fritz. She never married, but from the looks of the photograph, she enjoyed the hat fashion of the day. There were several millinery shops in town during her lifetime. William was the village president and served two years as the justice of the peace. Rena was a music teacher, pianist, and organist. She also lived in Colby and Stanley, Wisconsin. She is buried in Oakwood Cemetery. (Courtesy of the Weyauwega Public Library.)

ELIZABETH CRANE. Elizabeth Crane was the first Weyauwega High School valedictorian in 1889. At graduation, the class motto, "onward and upward," was wrought in pink roses and syringa hanging above the platform. The class flower was the pink carnation; class colors were pink and white. She said: "Indeed we really expected to get somewhere and nobody disillusioned us!" The school board consisted of Charles M. Fenelon, Tom Wilson, and her father, Wilder W. Crane. (Courtesy of the Weyauwega Public Library.)

WILLIAM BAUER. William Bauer (1839–1907) was born in Germany and settled in Weyauwega in 1866. He started a furniture store, in the same location as the Spot Tavern, with different types of furniture, pianos, and sewing machines. An undertaker, he made his own coffins. William married Hannah Beuke, and they had five children. William was the village president in 1884 and served for 11 terms. Hannah died in 1914. They are buried at Oakwood Cemetery. (Courtesy of the Weyauwega Public Library.)

FRITZ BAUER. Fritz Bauer (1883–1966), son of William, handled the Bauer store in Fremont, Wisconsin. It was about six miles south of Weyauwega. He was the undertaker there and took over the Bauer store in Weyauwega, running it as a furniture store and funeral home for 50 years. (Courtesy of the Weyauwega Public Library.)

MRS. MARY E.V. SORLEY. Mary Sorley (1856–1903) left Neenah, Wisconsin, in 1886. She started a music-and-drugstore in Weyauwega in January 1890. She handled only the finest goods in a 20-by-50-foot building on Main Street. She was a Sunday school teacher at the Presbyterian church, where she sang in the choir. Her sons were Stanley and Walter. She is buried in Oakwood Cemetery. (Courtesy of the Weyauwega Public Library.)

WILLIAM A. SPRINGER. William Springer developed the Wolf River apple, a large apple that is perfect for pies. In September 1880, Springer demonstrated a "monster apple" of the Wolf River variety weighing 21 ounces. Springer planted the first apple tree in 1851, and the first apples were harvested in 1854. In 1852, Springer witnessed the funeral of Menominee chief Wau-ke-john. (Courtesy of the Weyauwega Public Library.)

DEFOREST AND CELIA HAYWARD. The Haywards were famous as the superintendents and matrons of the Waupaca County Asylum—positions they held for 31 years. On April 2, 1902, Mr. and Mrs. Cyrus M. Hayward were elected superintendent and matron of the asylum. He served until January 1913; she served until March 1915. Their son Deforest C. Hayward and his wife, Celia, took over the jobs. Deforest died in 1944 and was buried in Lakeside Cemetery in Waupaca. (Courtesy of the Weyauwega Public Library.)

BERNICE POTTER. Bernice Potter was the daughter of Herbert W. Potter (1855–1932) and Mary Emily Gumaer (1860–1929). Her sister was Ruth M. Potter (1886–1939), who married Raymond A. Hutchinson (1886–1939). Bernice married Raymond's brother Hubert Hutchinson. (Courtesy of the Weyauwega Public Library.)

HENRY STIER. Henry Stier (1826–1898) was born in Prussia. Henry and his wife, Christiana, came to Weyauwega with their three children in 1867. He was a shoemaker and worked in the store of Reif and Ogden. He started Stier's Hall on West Main Street. Herman Anklam Sr. leased the business from Henry and later bought it. Stier moved on to farming on the southeast border of the village. He is buried in Oakwood Cemetery. (Courtesy of the Weyauwega Public Library.)

LOUISA GRUBB. Louisa, the daughter of William Bauer and wife of Edward F. Grubb, is shown in a surrey. In 1910, Edward F. Grubb, Dr. E.H. Jones, and Wilder Crane made an application for the charter of a new bank, the Farmers & Merchants Bank. Edward Grubb later served as the president of the bank. This photograph was taken in front of the Ritchie House. (Courtesy of the Weyauwega Public Library.)

A.J. RIECK. In 1906, Albert J. Rieck (1868–1959) worked for C.F. Crane as the editor of the *Weyauwega Chronicle*. By 1911, he became the owner of the *Chronicle*. He married Anna Ohen, and they had three children. He was on the Selective Service Board during World War II, and on the county fair board. In 1940, he retired after 35 years. He is buried in Oakwood Cemetery. (Courtesy of the Weyauwega Public Library.)

ANITA ROMON. Anita Romon was a librarian for 43 years at the Weyauwega Public Library. She categorized the day-to-day published materials that became the prime resource for this book. Anita secretly was Santa's (her husband, Mel) secretary, answering children's letters starting in 1936. She furnished the altar flower arrangements for the Presbyterian church for almost 40 years. Mel sold popcorn and cookies after becoming blind. (Courtesy of the Weyauwega Public Library.)

GROUP AT THE MOODY HOUSE. This group of ladies from Weyauwega is on East Main Street at the George Moody house around 1920. In the background is the Catholic church. D.E.H. Johns built the house in 1893 at 213 East Main Street. Two of the girls in the photograph are Goldie Cohen (far left) and Marion Hesler (far right), a high school teacher. Marion married Harold Clark. (Courtesy of the Weyauwega Public Library.)

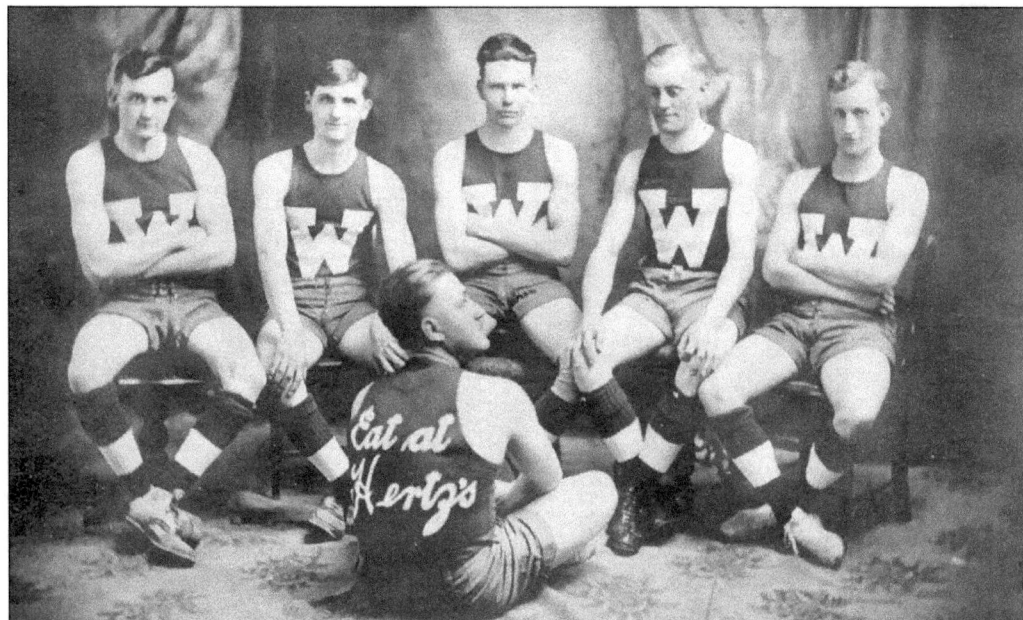

BOYS' SEMIPROFESSIONAL BASKETBALL TEAM, 1915. Home games were held at Whitney Hall on the Public Square on Mill Street. Sitting on the floor is Fred Hertz; sitting in chairs are, from left to right, Harry Hertz, Alvin Schutz, Linden "Dutch" Wall, William Richter, and Steve Carroll. This was not the high school team but a semiprofessional team. Games were held at various towns like New London, Neenah, and Menasha. Alvin Schutz practiced law in Weyauwega. (Courtesy of Keith Wall.)

OWNERS OF THE POST DRUGSTORE. Lorenzo D. Post followed his father into business. He had a soda fountain installed in 1882. Pictured are, from left to right, Mrs. Post, Hal Post, Bessie Post, and Lorenzo D. Post. Other businesses at the time included Jacob Becker's cooper business, Fred Wall's delivery business, John Whitney's furniture business, Libby Ogden's millinery shop, Reas's livery stable, Jerome Crocker's basket factory, and Mathias Munsch's cooper business. (Courtesy of the Weyauwega Public Library.)

TAGGART AND PATCHIN FAMILIES. Seated at center is George W. Taggart Sr. Others are, from left
to right, (first row) Melvin Patchin (Hannah's son) and his wife; (second row) siblings George W.
Taggart Jr., Hannah (Taggart) Patchin, Robert Taggart, and Hannah's unidentified friend. Bass
built the house on the corner of South Mill and South Streets around 1848. Taggart Sr. purchased
the house in 1857, which remained in the family for more than 75 years. There is a widow's walk
at the top of the house. From here, an eye could be kept on people coming from Gills Landing.
(Courtesy of the Weyauwega Public Library.)

McCalls. The McCall family lived on East High Street near Oakwood Cemetery. Pictured are, from left to right, (first row) Dollie, Hattie, and Katie; (second row) Kirk and John McCall. Their father, Alex McCall, was a pioneer merchant in Weyauwega before Civil War. He operated the Weyauwega Post Office from 1885 to 1890 with W.H. Weed as the postmaster. Alex, a carpenter and lumber dealer, clerked in his father John C. McCall's store, Weisbrod and McCall. (Courtesy of the Weyauwega Public Library.)

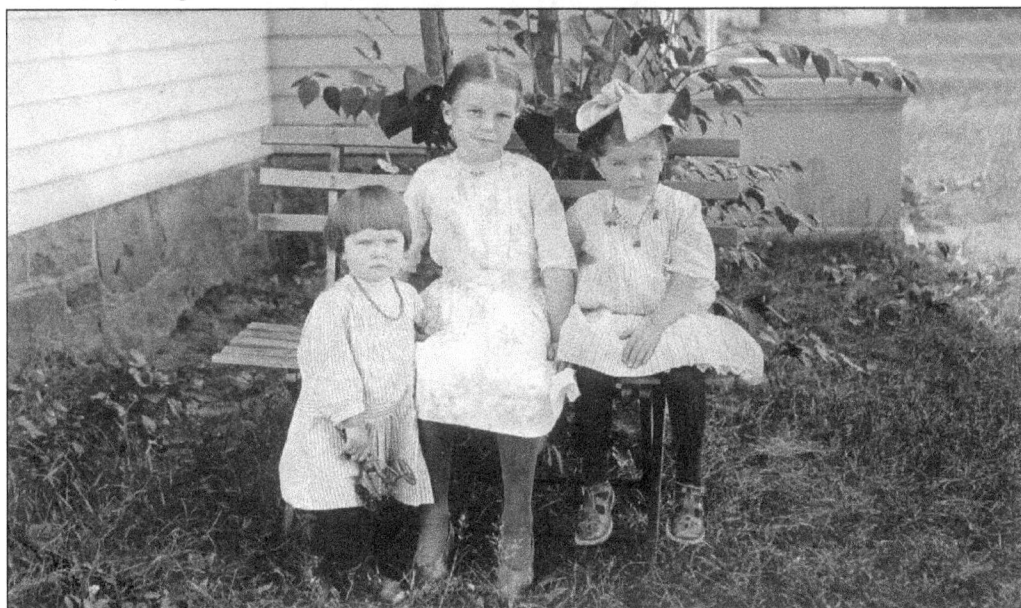

Harden Girls. The daughters of Fred and Nora (Neidhold) Harden are shown in their yard on Parker Street. They are, from left to right, Neida, Mildred, and Marie. Parker Street is only a block south of where the town square was originally located. Fred Harden had a grocery store on Main Street. (Courtesy of the Weyauwega Public Library.)

HATTIE REGAL WEDDING. The Regal family has been in the Weyauwega area for a long time. The photographer named on this image, H.D. Denninger, was born in 1851 in Berlin, Germany. His father was a Lutheran pastor. H.D. Denninger graduated from Watertown (Wisconsin) High School and taught 20 years in parochial schools. Denninger arrived in Weyauwega in 1895 and established his photography studio. He was elected mayor of Weyauwega in 1915. (Courtesy of Ethel Doede.)

SCHEEL FAMILY RESIDENCE. Pictured are G.D. Scheel family members and friends in front of their residence. This may have been after a Sunday school session on the front lawn of the Scheel home. (Courtesy of the Weyauwega Public Library.)

HANNAH PATCHIN'S 90TH BIRTHDAY PARTY, AUGUST 22, 1933. Pictured are, from left to right, (seated) Addie Neidhold, Ida Meyers, Paula Uttormark, Olla Weisbrod, Frances Gerguson, and Emma Jones (partially visible); (kneeling) Mrs. Charles Ritchie and Mrs. Stevens; (standing) Mrs. George Miller, Mrs. George Haire, Mrs. Charles Baldwin, Mrs. Stearns, Ruth Weisbrod, Mrs. Lions, Mrs. Patchin, Martha Ritchie, Kate Ritchie, Dr. Ida Hunt, Nora Harden, Florence Baldwin, Mrs. Van Vorst, and Mary Springer. Hannah Patchin was remembered as a prominent leader in the Women's Christian Temperance Union and an advocate for women's rights. (Courtesy of the Weyauwega Public Library.)

ABE RICE READY FOR A RIDE. Charles A. Rice, born in New Jersey, arrived in Weyauwega in 1859 at the age of 18. He was a skilled performer on most stringed instruments, a gunsmith, and cabinetmaker. His first wife, Helen Tew, had a son, Arthur A. His second wife, Clarissa Lillie, had a son, Orrin, and daughter, Mundie. Pictured are, from left to right, Arlene, Lillian, Harriette, and Abe, children of Arthur and grandchildren of Charles. Charles died on November 28, 1908. He is buried in Waupaca. (Courtesy of the Weyauwega Public Library.)

BALLARD HOUSE. Adam and Emma (Jane Baker) Ballard's house on the corner of East Alfred and East Streets looked like a full house. They had nine children. Adam Ballard worked as the head butter maker at the Baldwin Creamery. Their daughter Lettie Mae married Harry Farley, the son of George Farley of New York. Another child in the photograph was Royal, who married Jo Wilson. (Courtesy of James Waid.)

POST FAMILY IN THE SNOW. Post family members are seen in their yard near the town square. This was taken around 1915. (Courtesy of the Weyauwega Public Library.)

GENE HENRY AND SON PHIL, C. 1908. Gene Henry, born in Pennsylvania, was Jeannie Wilcox's brother. He died at the age of 84 on November 23, 1913. He was a farmer and died of toxemia. Dr. Jeffery was the attending doctor. The little boy in this photograph was his son Phillip. (Courtesy of the Weyauwega Public Library.)

ENOS CLARK. Enos Clark was known for carrying the mail from the depot to the post office and vice versa. Clark was also a farmer. At the age of 71, he died on February 23, 1926, of gangrene under the care of Dr. Chandler. (Courtesy of the Weyauwega Public Library.)

KYES CHILDREN. Sitting on a swing in the backyard are the children of Dr. Kyes, the dentist. Unfortunately, they are unidentified. Another dentist, in 1886, was F.E. Judson. His office was located above the Post store and he advertised false teeth for $8 a set. (Courtesy of the Weyauwega Public Library.)

WILLIAM F. GUMAER AND EDMUND A. FORDYCE. William Gumaer (left) and Edmund Fordyce are shown in a c. 1883 tintype. Edmund was an ambitious kid. He went around town to get subscriptions to raise enough money to have a toboggan slide built. Edmund lived in Iowa during his high school years. He was the son of attorney John Fordyce. William was the son of another early settler, William Gumaer. (Courtesy of the Weyauwega Public Library.)

41

BEHIND THE WILCOX STORE. Katie Wilson is on the top step behind the Wilcox Store. Henry F. Wilcox, age 51, was born in Wisconsin and was a general merchant. His father was Willard; his mother was Eliza. Henry died at the age of 51 on January 17, 1913, of a stroke. He is buried at Hobart Cemetery just out of town on County Road O. Katie is thought to have been the daughter of Thomas Wilson, the banker. (Courtesy of the Weyauwega Public Library.)

ADAM BALLARD FAMILY. Pictured are, from left to right, (first row) Adam and Emma, with children Adelle, Lucille, and Lettie May; (second row) Arthur, Royal, and Leslie. Emma was the daughter of Simon Baker. The Ballards were married on October 17, 1868. She died at the age of 83 in 1931 at Adelle's home, three years after her husband. They are buried in the Oakwood Cemetery in Weyauwega. (Courtesy of James Waid.)

A.L. AND ADA HUTCHINSON. Attorney Alfred L. Hutchinson, or A.L., as he was known, was the son of Debius and Mary Hutchinson and was born in Weyauwega in 1859. He moved to the village of Weyauwega from a farm in 1882 and was appointed postmaster that year. He developed the post office from a fourth-class office to a state-of-the-art one. In 1886, he became the editor of the *Weyauwega Chronicle*. He was elected secretary of the fair association and had full management of the fair. The fair became one of the largest in northern Wisconsin, with the best in horse racing. He called a special meeting for a vote on organizing a high school. Hutchinson is shown with his wife, Ada Baldwin. (Courtesy of Ray Hutchinson.)

LADIES OF WEYAUWEGA. The ladies in this November 2, 1899, photograph are, from left to right, Grubb, Haire, Borham, Weed, Van Epps, and Fenelon. The photograph was taken in front of the Peter Van Epps home on Sumner Street. (Courtesy of the Weyauwega Public Library.)

POST GIRL ON THE HAMMOCK. Seated on the hammock are Elizabeth "Bess" Post and an unidentified friend on the side lawn of the Post home on the corner of southeast Parker and Mill Streets. (Courtesy of the Weyauwega Public Library.)

44

BIRTHDAY PARTY, FEBRUARY 1909. The following women attended a birthday party in 1909, from left to right, (first row) Stier, Dahms, Lapoint, and Petersen; (second row) Auger, Puffer, Ballard, Rossey, Olson, and Rohn ?. Two of the babies were Charles and Alice Petersen. (Courtesy of the Weyauwega Public Library.)

PETER VAN EPPS FAMILY, 1927. Peter L. Van Epps was born in New York in 1845, served four years in the Union Army with the 44th New York Infantry, and was left for dead for two days at Gaines Mills. He came to Weyauwega in 1868, worked as a farmer, and dealt in meats. He married Abigail Puffer in 1868, and they had three children. Peter was the village marshal, the deputy sheriff, and an early commander of the Grand Army of the Republic Andrew Chambers Post No. 180. Their house was on East Sumner Street. (Courtesy of Mary Van Epps Schultz.)

HUTCHINSON BOYS. These brothers, sons of A.L. Hutchinson, were photographed around 1910. They are, from left to right, Hubert, Alfred, Ray, Harold, and Earle. (Courtesy of Ray Hutchinson.)

FRANK HAFFNER. Frank Haffner is dressed for the Horse-and-Buggy Days event. Frank, born in 1894, was known for many years as "Mister Fair." He was a bookkeeper for the Evanswood Cheese Factory, but he was most known as a horse judge for the Waupaca County Fair. Haffner was the fair secretary for nine years, town chairman for eight years, and Evanswood School clerk for 18 years. He was instrumental in getting the old Baxter Schoolhouse saved and moved to the city park. He was active in the Ss. Peter and Paul Catholic Church. (Courtesy of the Weyauwega Public Library.)

GUSTAV PIGORSCH. Gustav Pigorsch was noted for building ships in a bottle. He and his wife, Henrietta, are shown with one of his creations. Gustav lived from 1871 to 1955. Henrietta (Pufahl) lived from 1869 to 1951. (Courtesy of the Weyauwega Public Library.)

MARTY VEY. Marty Vey was a lifelong resident of Weyauwega. He was born on May 16, 1911, and died on May 31, 2006, at the age of 95. Marty was the son of Louis and Bertha Vey. Marty was remembered as the owner of the Fairway Store on Main Street for more than 60 years. Marty once said, "They all made a living" when talking about the 15 or so stores competing with each other in the 1930s. He was a member of St. Peter Evangelical Lutheran Church. Marty is buried in Oakwood Cemetery. (Courtesy of the Weyauwega Public Library.)

47

DR. J.F. CORBETT AND HIS WIFE, HATTIE. Dr. Corbett was born in Wisconsin in 1856 and graduated from the medical department of Western Reserve University of Cleveland, Ohio, in 1880, the same year he married Hattie Barber. For 12 years, he served as surgeon for Wisconsin Central Railway. In 1883, Corbett's office was located over J.D. Puffer's drugstore. Corbett was the business manager for the *Weyauwega Chronicle* from 1883 to 1886. His drug company's name was Hardy & Corbett, later known as Bennett & Corbett, from 1888 to 1894. (Courtesy of the Weyauwega Public Library.)

DR. E.H. JONES AND HIS WIFE, MARTHA, 1890. Dr. Edward H. Jones was most known for delivering approximately 2,600 babies in Weyauwega during a 50-year span. He had the Exchange Building built for his office and, later, the Wolf River Telephone Company. The building on the corner of Mill and Main Streets still stands. He was the president of the Farmers & Merchants Bank and the first president of the Lions Club. Martha, his second wife, was in style with a great looking hat. Jones used a Model T with skis on the front in the winter. He was a physician at Waupaca County Asylum from 1902 until 1947. He had two children, Alice and Stuart, by his first wife. (Courtesy of the Weyauwega Public Library.)

DR. THOMAS LANGER. Thomas Langer was thought to be the first doctor in Weyauwega; however, not much is known about him. He was the first secretary and charter member of the Free and Accepted Masonic Lodge No. 82. This is his pre–Civil War Masonic photograph. (Courtesy of the Weyauwega Public Library.)

DR. JAMES S. WALBRIDGE. Dr. James S. Walbridge worked his way through the University of Michigan and received his degree in 1874. He came to Weyauwega in 1874 and established his medical practice here. His brother F.E. Walbridge joined his practice in 1880. This is Dr. James S. Walbridge's Masonic photograph. (Courtesy of the Weyauwega Public Library.)

Birds Eye View of Weyauwega, Wis.

BIRD'S–EYE VIEW OF WEYAUWEGA. The lower right corner shows the George Moody house at 218 East Main Street. Moody came to Weyauwega in 1912 to manage the Weyauwega Milling Company. He married Mary Reese. Moody was an official in the Weyauwega Telephone Company and Weyauwega Electric Lighting Company. Dr. Correy started a hospital here in 1934 and stayed until 1945. Dr. Hudson took over and ran the hospital from 1945 to 1949. The brick house at the left, 214 East Main Street, was built by Hank Crane Sr. in 1890 and later purchased by A.L. Hutchinson. (Courtesy of the Weyauwega Public Library.)

DR. JONES WITH FIRST BABY AND LAST DELIVERY. This photograph was taken at the 50th anniversary of Dr. E.H. Jones's medical practice for Dr. Jones Day, in Weyauwega. Dr. Jones is shown with his first delivery, Belle Pike of Stevens Point, and his latest delivery, Percy Seymour Tesch of Pine River. Dr. Jones was a member of the Equitable Reserve Association and the medical examiner for the Equitable Reserve Association Insurance Company. Jones died on March 14, 1948, at the age of 89. He was a master Mason since 1885. (Courtesy of the Weyauwega Public Library.)

WILLIAM C. POTTER AND JAMES S. POTTER.
The Potter family was a moving force in
Weyauwega. Herbert W. Potter ran a dry goods
store on Main Street. William and James
Potter were Masons; James was made a master
Mason in June 1859. These photographs were
taken from the Masonic lodge album. It is
not known how these two men were related.
(Courtesy of the Weyauwega Public Library.)

Three

BUSINESSES

BENNETT & MYERS FUNERAL HOME. The (Abijah) Bennett Store was built in 1895 on Mill Street. Founder Abijah Bennett established his funeral and furniture business in 1886. His son, Harry, took over the business in 1913. He was not a mortician. Pliney F. Myers sold furniture in the Bennett Store with Harry. Arnold J. Kopitzke and Hugo Zuberbier were the morticians. On June 11, 1932, the two opened their own funeral home on North Mill Street at the old Crane house. Harry's house on West Main Street was built by Julius Strochein in 1908 for $3,290. Truman Harrigan bought the house and funeral business, running it until about 1980. (Courtesy of the Weyauwega Public Library.)

BLACKSMITH SHOP. This is the blacksmith shop of E. Ensign. To the left is the store of Peter L. Van Epps. Ensign and Van Epps were brothers-in-law and partners, but they dissolved their partnership in January 1884. Ensign continued the business. Following Ensign's death in 1903, Fred Stroschein purchased the blacksmith shop and tools. (Courtesy of the Weyauwega Public Library.)

INTERIOR VIEW OF THE BLACKSMITH SHOP. This is the interior view of the blacksmith shop of F. Stroschein & Son, the old blacksmith shop of E. Ensign. Shown are, from left to right, Henry Stroschein, the owner, and blacksmith Olaf Sky. Weyauwega has had several other blacksmiths, including Dauber, Morehouse, Smith, Kosanke, and Hennig. (Courtesy of the Weyauwega Public Library.)

HUTCHINSON HOTEL. This postcard view is the oldest of the Hutchinson Hotel, built by A.L. Hutchinson in 1899. The hotel was constructed on the site of the old Woods Hotel, first known as the LaDow House. The third floor was removed after a fire. Note the horse barn on west side. (Courtesy of Florence Oehlke.)

RICHARD DOST TIN SHOP. This photograph shows Dick Dost in front of his tin shop, which was located on North Mill Street on the east side of the millpond. This spot is now a parking lot. (Courtesy of the Weyauwega Public Library.)

LAKEVIEW HOTEL. Robert Baxter built the American House, later named the Lakeview Hotel, on North Mill Street in May 1850. Weyauwega's first town meeting was held here on April 6, 1852. Peter and Maria Bozile later owned the hotel; their daughter Mary married H.S. Keeney in 1883. Mary was born on February 17, 1859, in New York. The Woodman Hall and a blacksmith shop were next to this hotel. It was torn down in 1945 and replaced by Clarence Radtke's bowling establishment. (Courtesy of Florence Oehlke.)

BORNGESSER HOUSE. The Borngesser House was first known as the LaDow House when Robert Baxter and Charles Haire built it in 1852. It later became the Tarbell House, Borngesser, and then the Woods Hotel. It burned down in 1897. The boardinghouse was located at the southwest corner of Mill and Main Streets. In addition to having had many owners and names, this structure also had a prime location downtown. Watterston's store was across the street. (Courtesy of the Weyauwega Public Library.)

EXCHANGE BUILDING. Dr. E.H. Jones built the Exchange Building in 1895 on the site previously occupied by the Tibbetts' Weyauwega House, which burned down in 1869, and William Woods's two-story frame building. It was called the Exchange because it housed Weyauwega's first telephone office on the second floor until 1934. The public library was organized in 1912 and was first housed on the second floor. Dr. Jones had his office on the second floor. Brusberg and Froelich of New London were the contractors. Leone Paap worked for Dr. Jones as well as the telephone company. (Courtesy of the Weyauwega Public Library.)

EXCHANGE BUILDING ADDITION. This photograph shows the Exchange Building after its addition. Power poles and lines are also visible in this photograph compared to the one above. In 1932, the building's name was changed to the Salzman Building after Sam Salzman and his wife, Fannie, moved their grocery and dry goods business there. Their store was previously located on North Mill Street. Sam Salzman served as the last village president before Weyauwega became a city in 1939. (Courtesy of Kim J. Heltemes.)

POTTER STORE. This is the interior of the H.W. Potter and Company store from the 1870s. The store's competition was the Post family's store. In all, Lorenzo and Joseph Post started three stores, the shanty at the southwest corner of Mill and Main Streets, the store on the southeast corner of Mill and Main Streets (pictured below), and the one on the north side of East Main Street. Their last store was a drugstore that was started in 1857. (Courtesy of the Weyauwega Public Library.)

POST STORE INTERIOR, 1908. This photograph was taken for the Post drugstore's 51st anniversary (1857–1908); the store was on the north side of Main Street. Pictured are, from left to right, Lorenzo D. Post, Mrs. Post, Mrs. Bellinger, unidentified, Elizabeth (Post) LaBudde holding a tray of biscuits, two unidentified, William Reese, and Irving Scheel. After running the business for 61 years, Lorenzo D. Post sold his store to John Look of Sheboygan, Wisconsin, in 1928. In 1934, Look sold to Don Shelp and Clayton Stearns. (Courtesy of the Weyauwega Public Library.)

HAIRE AND HARDEN STORES, EAST MAIN STREET. East Main Street hosted several grocery and dry goods stores. George Haire Groceries and Dry Goods store is shown on the left and Fred A. Harden Groceries and Dry Goods is on the right. Dr. Miller had an office above the Harden store. (Courtesy of the Weyauwega Public Library.)

HAIRE STORE INTERIOR. George Haire moved into a new building, shown, erected by George M. Haire and Edward W. Brown in 1892. E.W. Brown is standing on the left, and George Haire and Elizabeth Pope are on the right. (Courtesy of the Weyauwega Public Library.)

MARY SORLEY AND WILCOX STORES, 1905. Mary Sorley sold fresh drugs, patent medicines, paints, wallpaper, school supplies, glassware, fine china, confectionery products, and fruits. Henry F. Wilcox was a general merchant. (Courtesy of the Weyauwega Public Library.)

MARY E.V. SORLEY STORE INTERIOR. Shown is the interior of Mary Sorely's drugstore. E.B. Sorley, her husband, came to Weyauwega in 1886; he was a druggist at the Puffer Drugstore. He started a drugstore in 1888 and took care of that part of the store while Mary filled out the rest of the store with only the finest items. (Courtesy of the Weyauwega Public Library.)

BALDWIN CREAMERY INTERIOR. This is the interior of the Baldwin Creamery. Unidentified men are near the butter churns as they sit idle. Note the belts that run the equipment from the overhead power shaft. (Courtesy of the Weyauwega Public Library.)

BALDWIN CREAMERY OFFICE. C.P. Baldwin and O.D. Sanders on North Mill Street organized the Baldwin Creamery in 1892. The creamery had a capacity of 8,000 pounds of butter per week. Addie Neidhold, sister-in-law of grocer Fred Harden, worked in the creamery office. Martha Ritchie, a teacher, became a bookkeeper for the Creamery. Her body lay in state at the home of her brother Charles, and the funeral was held at the Presbyterian church. (Courtesy of the Weyauwega Public Library.)

GEBAUERS OPERA HOUSE. Gebauers Opera House, located on the east side of North Mill Street, was built and owned by Pauline Gebauer and her husband. From 1884 to 1889, it was a saloon and dance hall. It was 40 by 60 feet and opened in October 1884 with a big dance; in its opening year, the hall offered the first place to roller skate in town. It was sold to William Bauer in 1889. (Courtesy of the Weyauwega Public Library.)

BAUER STORE. The Bauer Store, started by William Bauer, conducted a furniture and funeral business for three generations. They built coffins until the railroad made it easier for them to offer factory-made items at a cheaper price. Fritz Bauer, William's son, took over the business in 1907. Over 4,000 funerals were held in their first 60 years of business. The Mill Street store building was destroyed by fire in 1972. By then the business had moved to Main Street, and the old building was used for storage. (Courtesy of Florence Oehlke.)

VIEW FROM WEYAUWEGA, WIS.

LAKESIDE CREAMERY. T.W. Rohdes was the proprietor of the Lakeside Creamery at the corner of Wisconsin and Mary Streets in 1903. The creamery's office is on the right. Fred Zeichert was in charge of the cheese factory and later became the owner and changed it to Star Cheese Factory in 1924. Marv Strey later bought it out in 1947. (Courtesy of Florence Oehlke.)

OPERA HOUSE. The opera house cost $20,000 to build in 1915. The opening night was September 2, 1915, with a dance and two dinners. Built by George Gerold (1858–1931), a retired farmer, it could accommodate 412 people. George Gerold was married to Catherine. His funeral was at the opera house, and he is buried in Oakwood Cemetery. In 1923, the Gerold Opera House served as a temporary classroom for the local school while the school was being rebuilt after a fire. The building is on the Wisconsin Architecture and History Inventory. (Courtesy of the Weyauwega Public Library.)

FIRST NATIONAL BANK. The First National Bank was organized in 1905. R.H. Edwards and E.L. Kosanke served as presidents and H. Koehler as the vice president. E.M. Proctor, R.W. Johnson, and A.L. Kosanke were the cashiers. Wedhde was a teller. There were several dentist offices upstairs, including Ostermeir and Kyes. Dr. Lloyd Maasch had an office in the upper level of this building before starting a clinic. Dr. Maasch's wife was Patricia. (Courtesy of Florence Oehlke.)

BANK. Weed, Gumaer & Co. built the bank on the northeast corner of Mill and Main Streets in 1856. Dr. E.H. Jones was the president, and T.F. Wilson was the cashier. Its vice presidents were W.W. Crane, Ben Wiener, and L.D. Post. The bank building was destroyed by fire in 1903. Uttormark brothers cleared the debris and erected a large brick building housing the bank, and the Weisbrod hardware store was on the adjoining lot. The Weed, Gumaer & Co. bank was absorbed in 1910 by the Farmers & Merchants Bank (F&M Bank), which continued operating on this corner until 1954. Charlie Ritchie later served as the president of F&M Bank. The block also included the home of Dr. Corbett, the music store of Arthur Rice, and the drugstore of John Puffer. (Courtesy of the Weyauwega Public Library.)

ARTHUR KOEHLER HARDWARE STORE. Arthur Koehler is on the left in his North Mill Street hardware store about 1921–1922. Located on the Wisconsin Street corner, this was the Kosanke brothers' store from 1881 to 1915. Koehler ran the store with his father-in-law, Charles Bauer, shown on the right, from 1915 to 1935, when Otto Reek bought the store. Otto's son Leonard took over the business from 1959 to 2002. (Courtesy of the Weyauwega Public Library.)

REEK HARDWARE. The Reek Hardware store was located on the corner of Mill and Wisconsin Streets. Otto Reek purchased Arthur Koehler's hardware store in 1935. Otto's father came from Posen, Germany, in 1880 at the age of 25. He married Augusta Kapitzke in 1883. After the death of Otto in 1959, his son Leonard became the owner until May 2002. The customer in the photograph (left) has been identified as Ed Thiel. (Courtesy of the Weyauwega Public Library.)

WEYAUWEGA'S SECOND TRAIN DEPOT. This was the second depot. The first depot burned down in 1935, as was common with coal ash fires, dripping oil, and little firefighting equipment. The Wisconsin Central Railroad began the line in 1871, with Weyauwega getting its first train in 1872. The Green Bay & Western Line was started in 1896. It ran as the Soo Line through town for many years. People would sit around the counter at the depot to get the basketball scores as they were telegraphed from the opponent's location. (Courtesy of the Weyauwega Public Library.)

SPOT TAVERN. The Spot Tavern was located on the northeast corner of Main and Pine Streets. Women and children would enter through the back door if they wanted a bowl of chili. Pictured is Peter Boehg. William Bauer's first store was at this site before he moved to the North Mill Street location in 1889. Peter was a great-step-grandfather of Forrest Gettendorf. (Courtesy of the Weyauwega Public Library.)

QUADE AND SCHOENICK BREWERY, AROUND 1890. In April 1893, a half share ownership of the brewery passed to William Schoenick. The other owner was Gustav Frederick Quade (1857–1909), a brewer. On January 26, 1900, fire struck the brewery. Quade and Schoenick continued to brew in an 1855 building, and in July 1900, they announced dissolution of their partnership. Quade is buried in lot No. 422 at Oakwood Cemetery. (Courtesy of Florence Oehlke.)

POST OFFICE, C. 1915. The first post office in Weyauwega was established in 1850 with Benjamin Birdsall as postmaster. The post office occupied various locations on Main Street. By 1922, it was processing three railroad deliveries from each direction. This structure was built in 1915 on the south side of Main Street. The post office was later moved to its current location on Pine Street. (Courtesy of the Weyauwega Public Library.)

FAIRWAY STORE. Chris Nelson (1888–1937) started the Fairway Store on the east side of Main Street next to the opera house. The grocery was on the east side of the building, with a harness shop on the west side run by Paul Zimdars. Nelson worked at Henry Wilcox's store, his brother Peter's Nels Grocery, and at the Wiener brothers' Boston Store. Nelson married Elsie Vey in 1918. In 1920, he went out on his own as the Fairway Store. During Chris's funeral, all businesses in town were closed. (Courtesy of the Weyauwega Public Library.)

GERLACH GROCERY STORE. This photograph of Gerlach Grocery store in 1941 on West Main Street is a clear view of grocery store life in Weyauwega. From left to right are dentist Dr. Sarbor, Meta Arndt, Meta Miller, Melvin Gerlach, Ossie Prillwitz, Hank Schellin, Bill Borham, and Ed Gerlach. Dr. Sarbor had to wear the hearing apparatus, for he was nearly deaf. (Courtesy of Ossie and Gloria Prillwitz.)

WIGWAM SERVICE STATION. In 1929, Herman "Doc" Anklam employed Julius and Louie Stroschein to build this service station to resemble an Indian wigwam. The structure was originally covered with a plaster or concrete finish and colorfully painted, featured a smoke flap and sticks protruding at the peak. The original finish never cured properly and began deteriorating shortly after the wigwam was completed. The station, operated by Anklam and then Art Bork, was closed from 1933 to 1936. (Courtesy of the Weyauwega Public Library.)

WIGWAM SERVICE STATION LATER. Upstairs in the Wigwam was a small apartment rented to Dutch Ebert. In December, he sold Christmas trees next to the station. At the time of its existence, the Wigwam was adjacent to US Highway 10. In August 1936, Clarence and William Radtke leased the property for $15 per month. Soon after they began business there, the Radtkes had the structure shingled. The Wigwam service station building was dismantled in 1957. (Courtesy of the Weyauwega Public Library.)

Wigwam Service Station
Weyauwega, Wis.   R-1737

Wigwam Service Station
Weyauwega, Wis. — Highway 10

COUNTY ASYLUM BEING BUILT. Discussion for the asylum began in 1885, but local politics prevented selection of a site until 1900. The county finally agreed to purchase the Chase farm, in the town of Royalton, where the asylum was constructed. Construction finished in 1902, and it was a magnificent building. Here, the asylum is shown during the construction. It was recognized throughout the state as a model of its kind. In 1917, the asylum occupied 346 acres. (Courtesy of the Weyauwega Public Library.)

ASYLUM LATER. At its peak, the asylum handled 140 patients. The facility stopped mental illness care in 1974 and then closed. It had a working dairy farm that supported the patients with good meals. (Courtesy of the Weyauwega Public Library.)

Four

MILITARY

SOLDIERS MONUMENT BASE, 1901. Eri L. McNutt is second from the left with a bowler hat, and Reilly McNutt is driving the horses. Both lived just north of Clintonville. This team made the monument pictured, but when the Soldiers Monument needed a base, they used the base from this monument. The Soldiers Monument base and shaft are of Barre granite. The bronze statue atop the cylindrical shaft is more than life size. The memorial, unveiled by Margaret Bublitz, was dedicated on July 4, 1901, with the principal address being delivered by ex-governor Edward Scofield. The village board made an appropriation that, along with personal subscriptions, enabled the Soldiers Monument Society to advertise for bids. The contract for the monument was about $1,000. (Courtesy of Jeff Pockat.)

DEDICATION OF CIVIL WAR MONUMENT, 1931. This monument, donated by George W. Taggart Jr., honors the 1st Wisconsin Volunteer Cavalry, with which Taggart served. Ann Kingl Zimdars created the statue with Taggart's detailed instructions. The monument, dedicated on August 15, 1931, features a Morgan horse. Zimdars designed the statue with Anton Spaltoff sculpting it, and it was constructed and erected by Badger Monument Company of Milwaukee. Ed Gerlach and George Carpenter roasted an ox for the occasion. (Courtesy of the Weyauwega Public Library.)

LOVERS LANE. Lovers Lane was on South Mill Street with the Soldiers Monument in the middle of the intersection at Sumner Street. The Soldiers Monument Society was formed in 1887 to erect a monument in honor of Civil War veterans. A.L. Hutchinson was chosen president. Reverend Mackinnon gave the first dollar toward the fundraising. The Amateur Dramatic Society was organized to raise funds for the monument through numerous plays over the years. (Courtesy of the Weyauwega Public Library.)

ANDREW J. VAN EPPS. Andrew Van Epps (1829–1909), the son of James and Rosina Van Epps, was born in New York; he was engaged in the lumber business there until 1852, when he came to Weyauwega. He helped build the first sawmill for Gill & Tourtelotte, who sold it to Weed and Birdsall. Andrew was in Company C, 52nd Wisconsin Infantry, as a corporal. Later he was justice of the peace, assessor, president of the village, sheriff of Waupaca County, and in 1881, mayor of Waupaca. His funeral was one of the largest ever held in the city. He is buried in Oakwood Cemetery in lot No. 176, grave No. 12. (Courtesy of the Weyauwega Public Library.)

GEORGE W. TAGGART JR. Along with his brother Robert (born in 1851), George Taggart Jr. (1842–1933) operated a shoe store in town until Robert died in 1928. When the Civil War started, he joined the 1st Wisconsin Cavalry, Company M. He was mustered out in February 1865 as a commissary sergeant. He funded the creation of the Cavalry Monument. Late in life, George was struck by a car he did not know was coming because he was blind. (Courtesy of the Weyauwega Public Library.)

JOSEPH D. POST. Joseph Post, a Mason, was the son of Seth Post of Vermont. Joseph and his brother, Lorenzo L. Post, came to Weyauwega in 1851. Joseph was elected on the county board in 1852 as sealer of weights and measures, along with Robert Baxter, and owned the American House on North Mill Street in 1855. He enlisted in the 14th Wisconsin Infantry, died of wounds in 1862, and is buried in Oakwood Cemetery in lot No. 8. (Courtesy of the Weyauwega Public Library.)

WESLEY MESSENGER. Wesley Messenger was born on January 10, 1843. On September 10, 1861, Messenger, a Mason, enlisted into Company B, 14th Wisconsin Infantry. He rose through the ranks as corporal and sergeant and was mustered out on October 9, 1865. He did not live long after the war. Messenger died on June 12, 1867. A new marker has been installed on his grave in Oakwood Cemetery, lot No. 136, grave No. 7. (Courtesy of the Weyauwega Public Library.)

CIVIL WAR VETERANS. In no particular order are the following Civil War veterans: Peter Van Epps, Charles Goodnow, George Miller, Robert Taggart, ? Meyers, Van ?, Asa Worden, ? Schoeneck, Dave Wafler, John Almon, Adam Ballard, Charles Lawrence, George Stevens, Edward Vincent, and John Smith. Asa Worden was the major in Company B, 14th Wisconsin, and does not have a death date on his marker because he outlived the rest of his family. (Courtesy of the Weyauwega Public Library.)

LYMAN HOWARD. Lyman M. Howard was from Company C, 187th New York Infantry. This is a photograph from the Masonic Lodge No. 82 album. Howard was a Mason in Weyauwega. He is buried in Oakwood Cemetery in lot No. 65, grave No. 7. (Courtesy of the Weyauwega Public Library.)

EDRIC AND WILLIAM WESLEY STARKS.
Pictured are the Stark brothers, Edric on
the left and William Wesley on the right.
William served in the 12th Wisconsin
Infantry and died in a Nashville hospital.
He is supposedly buried there. William
may be the sheriff in the Gebauers Opera
House photograph on page 62. Edric served
in Company B of the 14th Wisconsin
Infantry and later served in Company G
of the reorganized 3rd Wisconsin Cavalry.
(Courtesy of John Irish and Kim J. Heltemes.)

**ADAM BALLARD, LORENZO BALLARD, AND
FRANK COLBY.** Cpl. Adam Monroe Ballard
(1845–1927), seated on the left, enlisted
in Company A, 42nd Wisconsin Infantry,
on August 13, 1864, and was mustered
out in 1865. Lorenzo, Adam's brother, is
standing. He served in Company A of the
8th Wisconsin Infantry. Frank Colby was
a friend of the Ballards. This photograph
shows the soldiers as they appeared on their
return home. (Courtesy of James Waid.)

COLUMBUS AND IDA CALDWELL. Columbus Caldwell (1830–1908) was born in New York. Caldwell came to Wisconsin in 1835 and married Mary Taggart, the daughter of George W. Taggart. On December 6, 1861, he enlisted in Company M of the 1st Wisconsin Cavalry, serving as the regimental quartermaster and as second lieutenant. In 1872 and 1873, he was elected to the Wisconsin legislature, became the superintendent of the Waupaca County Poor House in 1882, and in December 1887, took the job as the second commandant of the Wisconsin Veterans Home at King, Wisconsin. Ida, his second wife, was the matron at the home. Caldwell was buried at Oakwood Cemetery, with his first and second wives. (Courtesy of Kim J. Heltemes.)

CHARLES GOODNOW. Charles Goodnow was a Civil War veteran serving in Company K, 30th Wisconsin Infantry. A lapel pin from the Grand Army of the Republic can be seen on his coat. Goodnow is supposed to be one of the men in the Weyauwega Civil War veterans photograph on page 75. Goodnow was a miller in the Weed and Gumaer mill, a member of the first brass band, and the chief of Weyauwega's fire department. This is a Charles Lawrence Studio photograph. (Courtesy of the Weyauwega Public Library.)

HIRAM RUSSELL. Hiram Russell was a captain in Company B, 21st Wisconsin Infantry. He was wounded and taken prisoner during the Chickamauga campaign. Russell was discharged due to a disability because of the wound. This photograph of Russell was taken before the Civil War when he was a Mason at Weyauwega Masonic Lodge No. 82. (Courtesy of the Weyauwega Public Library.)

HENRY PEGRAM. The *Shawano County Reporter* in 1870 said Henry Pegram died at Weyauwega on May 30. He enlisted as a private in the 17th Wisconsin Infantry, Company K, in 1862 at Keshena, Wisconsin. His wife, No-ka-no, was a Native American. Pegram's father was a white man, and his mother, Mo-ke-che-won, was Menominee. Henry was listed as a deserter and lies in an unmarked grave in Oakwood Cemetery in Weyauwega. (Courtesy of the Weyauwega Public Library.)

SIMON BAKER. Simon W. Baker (1824–1892) was born in New York. In 1864, at 40 years of age, Simon enlisted in Company B of the 14th Wisconsin Volunteer Infantry. Simon was mustered out of service at Madison, Wisconsin, on October 22, 1865. Baker was the father-in-law of Adam Ballard. He died by infection of the bowels. Dr. Corbett was the attending doctor. He is buried in lot No. 438, grave No. 12, at Oakwood Cemetery. (Courtesy of James Waid.)

Volney Shelley. Volney K. Shelley was born in 1830 in New York. After the death of his first wife, Catherine, he married her sister, Mary Elizabeth Deming, having seven children with her. He enlisted into Company B, 14th Wisconsin Infantry, and wore a locket with a photograph of his baby daughter, Abigail. Shelley stayed in Weyauwega until 1878, when he went to Mattoon, Wisconsin. He is buried in Oakwood Cemetery with a new military headstone. (Courtesy of Mary Werth.)

Golieb and Lizzie Weilandt. It seems that as the town got to the turn of the 20th century, photographs of soldiers became more rare. This photograph of Golieb Weilandt with his wife, Lizzie, shows Golieb as first sergeant when he was stationed in Wyoming. It was taken during the Indian Wars. Lizzie's maiden name was Elizabeth Schroeder. (Courtesy of Kim J. Heltemes.)

WALL IN WORLD WAR II. Linden "Dutch" Wall served from Weyauwega during World War I. He did not leave the states, like others from town who went overseas. (Courtesy of Keith Wall.)

JOSEPH POST MEMORIAL. Joseph Post's headstone reads, "Lieut. Joseph D. Post, Co. B, 14th Regiment Wisconsin Infantry, born December 25, 1825, wounded at the battle of Shiloh, Tenn. April 7, 1862, died of wounds at the Marine Hospital in Evansville, Ind. May 27, 1862." One of the Post children died in 1856 and is buried next to Joseph. In the years preceding May 1887, nearly half of the deaths were of children under five years old. (Courtesy of Kim J. Heltemes.)

ANDREW CHAMBERS'S MEMORIAL. Andrew B. Chambers enlisted into Company B, 14th Wisconsin, in 1861. In 1864, he was the company's second lieutenant. He came home to die on August 28, 1865. Chambers has a broken monument without his birth date on it. The Grand Army of the Republic Post No. 180 was named in honor of Chambers. Andrew Gasman was the first post commander. John Mack, P.L. Van Epps, and David Wafler were also post commanders. (Courtesy of Kim J. Heltemes.)

PVT. ERICK ARNDT. Erick Arndt, age 25, of Weyauwega, lost his life in World War I. He was killed in action on July 20, 1918, in France. He served in the 129th Infantry, 33rd Division. It was known as the Prairie Division. On December 31, 1919, the Weyauwega American Legion was chartered in his name as the Arndt-Bruley Post No. 176. (Courtesy of the American Legion Post No. 176.)

WEYAUWEGA BOYS AT CAMP. These unidentified men from Weyauwega are at Camp McClellan, Alabama, during their training for World War I. (Courtesy of the Weyauwega Public Library.)

PVT. HAROLD EDWARD "SPIKE" BRULEY. Private Bruley was killed in action while tending to a wounded soldier during battle at Normandy, France, on August 4, 1944. He was a member of the 134th Infantry as a medic. On August 25, 1944, he was posthumously given the Silver Star for gallantry while under fire from the enemy. The American Legion was named in his honor as the Arndt-Bruley Post No. 176. (Courtesy of the American Legion Post No. 176.)

HONOR ROLL. On August 7, 1943, when the Honor Roll was dedicated, 212 names were listed. Other names were added as the war progressed. Honored guests at the dedication ceremony were the parents or next-of-kin of the servicemen and women on the roll. Ben Wiener donated the site and the American Legion contributed the flagpole. The board, built by Julius Stroschein and painted by his son Alvin, was removed in 1952. The board has disappeared and has not been seen since. (Courtesy of the Weyauwega Public Library.)

Ossie Oswald Prillwitz. Ossie Prillwitz served in the Navy during World War II as a petty officer third class. He left for Guadalcanal aboard the USS *Chenango* and fought in the battles of Saipan, Tarawa, Admiralty Islands, Morotai, Halmahara, and Leyte Gulf. Ossie returned to the states in February 1945. He witnessed the first jet testing by Richard Bong and was discharged as aviation machinist first class. (Courtesy of Ossie and Gloria Prillwitz.)

Alvin "Pete" and Alice Neubauer. Alvin Neubauer enlisted in the Army in 1941 and was stationed at Camp Wolters in Texas. Later, he was transferred to the Aberdeen Proving Grounds at Baltimore, Maryland, where he met his wife, Alice Christine Clift. He achieved the rank of staff sergeant and was honorably discharged in 1945. (Courtesy of Jan Dahlke.)

AMERICAN LEGION. The old American Legion Building was on North Mill Street. The present Legion Post No. 176 eventually was rebuilt at that location in 1956. The post was formally organized in 1919; members used to meet at the Woods Hotel before using this location. (Courtesy of the Weyauwega Public Library.)

Five

SCHOOLS AND CHURCHES

PIONEER SCHOOL. The Pioneer School was built in 1854 to accommodate 250 students in five departments on East Main Street. It was the first school built at this location. In September 1879, Wisconsin law decreed that all children 7 to 15 years of age had to attend three months of school a year. A free high school was established in 1888. The first high school commencement was held in 1889. Charles D. Fenelon, the first high school principal until 1889, left to complete his first year at Rush Medical College to become a doctor. In 1891, he moved to Phillips, Wisconsin, for his practice. He married Sara M. Balch. Frank Grubb was another of the Pioneer principals. The Pioneer School was torn down in 1930. (Courtesy of the Weyauwega Public Library.)

BOTH SCHOOLS. In 1902, the wood framed Pioneer School was replaced with a square brick building next door. The cost of the new structure was $20,000, and the architect was Van Ryn of Milwaukee. The contractor was H.P. Knudson of Waupaca. Between 1889 and 1939, 717 students graduated. Four-year courses of study were divided into fall, winter, and spring terms each of three months duration. The brick school was rebuilt in 1924. When the present-day high school was built, it became the middle school. (Courtesy of Florence Oehlke.)

BURNED SCHOOL. This is a photograph of the brick school after it burned in 1923. The fire apparently started in the attic above the science room. About 45 tons of coal had just been delivered to the school's basement, which fueled the fire, so that the school was reduced to a shell in just an hour and a half. (Courtesy of the Weyauwega Public Library.)

O.M. SALISBURY. O.M. Salisbury was the
principal of Weyauwega High School
from 1891 to 1893. He was a University
of Wisconsin graduate. (Courtesy of
the Weyauwega Public Library.)

HIGH SCHOOL STUDENTS. High school students are seen standing in front of the school around
1914. Note the changes in the roofline and how much bigger the trees have grown. (Courtesy of
the Weyauwega Public Library.)

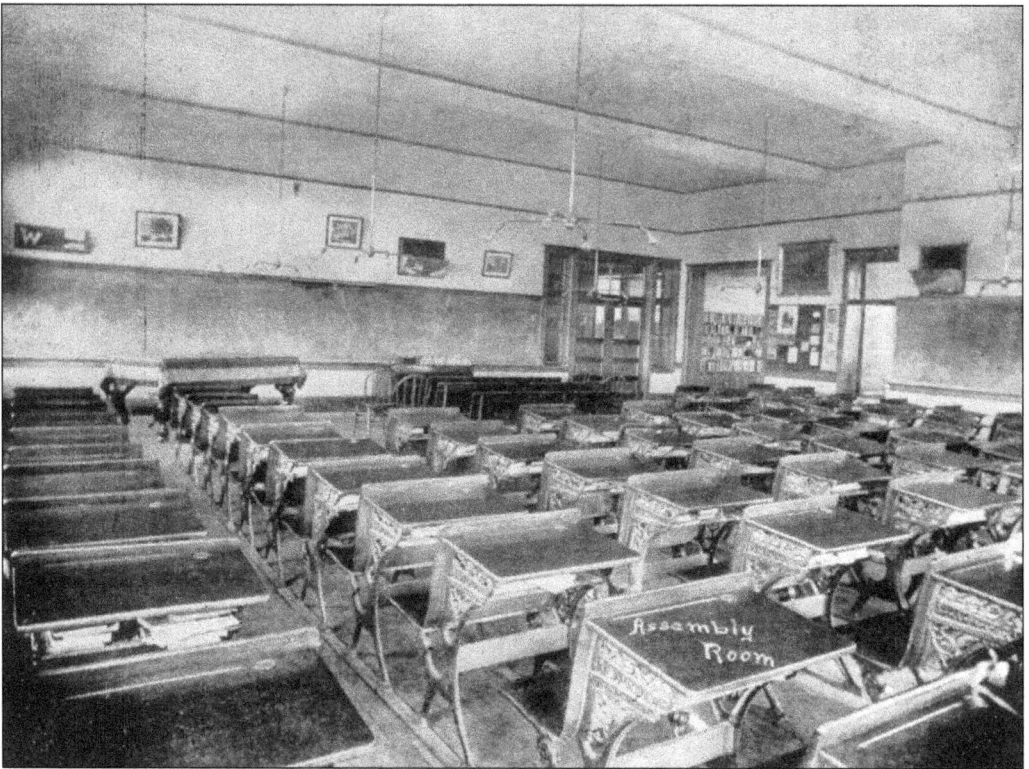

HIGH SCHOOL CLASSROOM. The high school's assembly room (homeroom) is pictured. Some of the elders in town remembered it still looking like that when they went to school. There were enough desks to seat 63 students. From here, the students went to their respective classes. (Courtesy of the Weyauwega Public Library.)

BOARD OF EDUCATION, 1910. The board of education in 1910 is shown here, with E.H. Jones, W.H. Weed, and David Wafler. Wafler was a Civil War veteran, having served in the 27th New York Infantry. (Courtesy of the Weyauwega Public Library.)

WILDER W. CRANE. Wilder W. Crane was a businessman in town. He purchased the building and stock of Potter and Company in 1884, but left the Potter and Company name on his store. He was on the school board. In 1889, his daughter Elizabeth and son Charles graduated from high school; Elizabeth was valedictorian. (Courtesy of the Weyauwega Public Library.)

GRADUATING CLASS, JUNE 17, 1892. The graduating class of 1892 includes, from left to right, (first row) Jean Harden, Lottie Zastrow, Will Wilcox, Mattie Myers, and Augusta Kneip; (second row) Lizzie Pope, Marion Clark, Hilda Bauer, Abbie Whitney, Francis Weisgerber, and Birdy Teal. (Courtesy of the Weyauwega Public Library.)

1910 GRADUATION CLASS. Divided into three panels are the students of the graduating class of 1910. In the left panel are, from left to right, (top row) Nels Johnson and Margaret Wilson; (middle row) Elwyn Grubb; (bottom row) Alma Hofett and Florence Cady. In the center panel are, from left to right, (top row) Flora Phillips, Paul Lewis, and Laura Larson; (bottom row) Floyd Neff, Pearl Jones, and Stella Hill. In the right panel are, from left to right, (top row) Nora Rohde and Elva Neff; (middle row) Irving Scheel; (bottom row) Laura Pagel and Laura Frihart. (Courtesy of the Weyauwega Public Library.)

HIGH SCHOOL TEACHERS, 1910. The high school faculty in 1910 included principal E.H. Miles and teachers Helen Chafin, Harriet Borham, and Helen Howe. (Courtesy of the Weyauwega Public Library.)

SCHOOL PHOTOGRAPH WITH
ADELLE BALLARD. Adelle Ballard
is on the far right in the second
row. The date of the class
photograph is unknown. Adelle
was the daughter of Adam Ballard.
(Courtesy of the James Waid.)

FRANK STARR AND SARAH CRANE.
Frank Starr was the principal at the
Weyauwega High School from 1895
to 1898. Sarah Crane, a daughter
of Wilder Crane, was a teacher
at the same school. (Courtesy of
the Weyauwega Public Library.)

1914 HIGH SCHOOL STUDENTS. Pictured around 1914 are Weyauwega High School students. From left to right are (first row) unidentified, Carolyn Bauer, Helen Hill, and Helen Sill; (second row) Mary Davidson, J. Volger, John Moody, Warren P. Blodgett, William Richter, Linden "Dutch" Wall, and unidentified. (Courtesy of the Weyauwega Public Library.)

FIRST AND SECOND GRADES, 1907. Standing along the blackboard are, from front to back, Alice Crane, Alfred Hutchinson, Arnold Zelzer, John McCall, Walter Timm, Kathryn O'Brien, and teacher Royal Green. From left to right across the room are, from front to back, (first row) Harold Clark, Elmer Dobbert, Clara Gerlach, Fred Martin, Esther Pagel, Amelia Neuschafer, Clarence Neidhold, and Robert Robertson; (second row) Irene Chick, Leslie Sherman, Maud Hazen, Roscoe Beyers, Melda Purchatzke, Dick Becker, Marjorie Freeman, Maude Farley, and Lidia Dobbert; (third row) Rea Beyers, Albert Niemuth, Elvers Zelzer, Kathryn Waterson, Edith Farley, Bob Keeney, Elsie Johnson, Albert Rieck, and Walter Sulmacher; (fourth) Lena Schultz, Leo Paap, Gladys Lorenz, Arden Judds, Irma Quade, and Isabella Andrews. This was in the old white school building. It is about the only known interior photograph of this school. (Courtesy of the Weyauwega Public Library.)

LITTLE RED SCHOOLHOUSE. The Baxter School was started by October 1861 when John and Maria Baxter bought half an acre for $30. The first teacher was Mary Schumacher. The school remained open until 1906. The building was used during World War I as a meeting hall. It is now called the Little Red Schoolhouse and is used as a museum; it is the third oldest schoolhouse in the state. It was moved to the city park in 1969. (Courtesy of Kim J. Heltemes.)

1914 BOYS' BASKETBALL TEAM. Members of the 1914 high school boys' basketball team are, from left to right, William Ritchie, Linden "Dutch" Wall, Alvin Schutz, Fred Hertz, Warren Blodgett, and Louis Sherburne. (Courtesy of the Weyauwega Public Library.)

HIGH SCHOOL GIRLS' BASKETBALL TEAM, 1898. The high school girls' basketball team from 1898 includes, from left to right, (first row) Blanche Wiggins, Chloe Baker, and Beatrice Uttormark; (second row) Josie Moyle, Cora Chase, Alice Jones, Alma Gerold, Harriet Chase, and Ruth Potter. (Courtesy of the Weyauwega Public Library.).

THE RABBITRY. The Rabbitry, pictured around 1920, was located behind the A.L. Hutchinson home on East Main Street. It was formerly used to raise rabbits for fur and meat. It was near the school, and it got a lot of attention from the children on their way home from school. (Courtesy of the Weyauwega Public Library.)

FIRST PRESBYTERIAN CHURCH
Congregation founded 1852
Church built 1854 by Debius Hutchinson
Manse built 1884

FIRST PRESBYTERIAN CHURCH. First Presbyterian Church on Alfred Street was organized in May 1852 at the home of Louis Bostedo with seven original members. Debius Hutchinson built the first church in 1854. The Rev. Alfred Gardner was their first regular minister. The original square belfry was replaced in 1884 with a conical steeple at a cost of $150. Charles Ritchie left a large amount of money to the Presbyterian church to erect a new church. Part of that money was set aside to construct the parsonage 30 years later. A new church was completed in 1951. (Courtesy of the Weyauwega Public Library.)

DEBIUS HUTCHINSON. Debius Hutchinson was born in 1810 in New York. He married Mary Baldwin, also of New York state. They moved to Weyauwega in 1853 and had a farm in Royalton. He built the First Presbyterian Church on a contract that stipulated he be paid $675. His son was A.L. Hutchinson. Debius died in 1894 and is buried in Oakwood Cemetery. (Courtesy of Ray Hutchinson.)

New Lutheran Church
Weyauwega Wis.

Copyright by H. Montgomery

ST. PETER EVANGELICAL LUTHERAN CHURCH. This is the St. Peter Evangelical Lutheran Church on West Main Street. It was organized February 25, 1872, and its first church was built on the north end of Lake Street the following year. The second church building, erected in 1888 at a cost of $2,500, seated 400 people. 600 people attended its dedication in October 1888. The third house of worship, a 50-by-117-foot brick structure, was dedicated in July 1910. It was completed at a cost of over $20,000 and has a seating capacity of 750. The membership of the congregation included 176 families. Until 1900, the first structure was used as a parochial school with 70 students. (Courtesy of Florence Oehlke.)

CATHOLIC CHURCH   WEYAUWEGA, WIS. 3R1099

CATHOLIC CHURCH POSTCARD. This is a postcard of the Ss. Peter and Paul Catholic Church, which was built on East Street in 1885 on land purchased by Archbishop Henni of Milwaukee in 1866. A parish report from 1893 lists 19 members with dues at $6 a year. A grand total of $138 was collected for the year. The priest from Hortonville, Wisconsin, served the parish. In 1955, the parish got its first full-time priest. (Courtesy of Kim J. Heltemes.)

METHODIST EPISCOPAL CHURCH. Weyauwega's Methodist church was formed on November 18, 1851. The church was built on the southeast corner of Mary and Sumner Streets in 1856. The female members, by means of sewing circles, saved money to build a parsonage for their preachers; it was located east of the church. R.S. Hayward was the first to serve the church in 1852. The church building was razed in the 1940s. (Courtesy of the Weyauwega Public Library.)

METHODIST SUNDAY SCHOOL. This photograph was taken in 1912 or 1913. Pictured are, from left to right, (first row) Claude Petersen, Nolan Olson, unidentified, Charles Petersen, and three unidentified; (second row) ? Wolfram, teacher Mayme Farley, Frances Sill, and unidentified. (Courtesy of the Weyauwega Public Library.)

BAPTIST CHURCH. The First Baptist Church, shown at upper right, was organized on September 9, 1854, and the meetinghouse was erected the following year. The first pastor was Peter Prink. It had a small membership in the early 1900s with 30 members. The church was located on East Alfred Street and was torn down in 1932. (Courtesy of the Weyauwega Public Library.)

HELEN THIEL. Helen Thiel is shown here in her confirmation dress. The confirmation was held at St. Peter Evangelical Lutheran Church. Her father was Daniel Thiel, a founding member of the church. (Courtesy of Florence Oehlke.)

Six

HOMES OF WEYAUWEGA

WATTERSON HOUSE. Pictured is the Watterson house. Watterson was an attorney and is shown in the photograph. Mr. Baldwin, owner of the Baldwin Creamery, later bought the house, so it became known as the Baldwin house. Most of these three-story homes erected during the town's early years are still standing. They are massive homes for a single family on what, at one time, was the Western frontier. (Courtesy of the Weyauwega Public Library.)

W.A. WEISBROD FAMILY, 1850s. In the early 1850s, Benjamin Birdsall built the home of W.A. Weisbrod on Ann Street. Weisbrod was born in Prussia in 1831, came to Weyauwega in 1855, and worked as a clerk. Next, he opened a boardinghouse, followed by a general merchandise store on Main Street, which burned down in 1869 but was rebuilt in 1870. He sold the meat market to Phil Sherman and Harry Baxter in 1890. W.A. married Augusta Schoenick and had six children. He retired in 1896 and died in 1898, when he was the village president. (Courtesy of the Weyauwega Public Library.)

WEED-CROCKER HOUSE. The Jacob Weed home was located at 310 South Mill Street. Weed's widow, Ann Elizabeth Gumaer Peddicord Weed, married Jerome Crocker in 1881. Crocker was one of the pioneer merchants of Weyauwega, selling dry goods, groceries, and general merchandise. Besides the store, Crocker owned a farm, a sawmill, and a basket factory. Charles Ritchie later bought the home. (Courtesy of the Weyauwega Public Library.)

FENELON HOUSE AND WEED HOME. Shown above in later years is the South Mill Street home of Charles M. Fenelon. It sits almost at the top of the hill overlooking the rest of the town. It was known for its immaculate landscaping while granddaughter Eunice S. Fenelon lived there. The house was built in 1855 and remained in the family until the mid-1990s. Charles Mercer Fenelon died in 1906 at the age of 75. He is buried in Oakwood Cemetery. Charles's mother was Sarah Balch, daughter of A.V. Balch, who was an 1851 settler, surveyor, insurance man, and state assemblyman in 1870. A.V. had a farm on the top of the hill overlooking Weyauwega. Below is the original Gumaer home on Mill Street bought by William Weed in 1894 at a cost of several thousand dollars. The home interior was redone in cherry and soft maple. (Above, courtesy of Kim J. Heltemes; below, courtesy of Ian Teal.)

FARLEY HOUSE, 1903. The Farley house was located across the corner from the telephone office on West Main Street. The Farleys and the Ballards were connected through marriage. B.P. Farley served as deacon, and George Farley was a Weyauwega Baptist church trustee. (Courtesy of the Weyauwega Public Library.)

H. TERHAR HOUSE. Not much is known about H. Terhar; however, this was his home. It was located on the corner of Mill and Parker Streets. (Courtesy of the Weyauwega Public Library.)

A.L. KOSANKE HOUSE. This is a view of West Sumner Street showing, from front to back, the homes of A.L. Kosanke, Higgins, Koehler, Bauer, Baldwin, and the Methodist church. In 1909, Kosanke entered the financial field at the First National Bank of Weyauwega. He married Mary Munsch in 1881. His parents were Ernest L. (1853–1895) and Wilhelmina (Paap) Kosanke. He was a blacksmith by trade. (Courtesy of the Weyauwega Public Library.)

HOUSE OF THE WEYAUWEGIAN. William C. Tompkins was the editor of the *Weyauwegian*, established in July 1855. This was Emma Haire's home on Pine Street, where the paper was printed. He had the printing case in front of the south window of the kitchen. He moved to an office on Main Street. Later papers were the *Herald*; the *Times*, published for eight years by F.W. Sackett; and finally, the *Chronicle*, founded by J.C. Keeney in 1877. (Courtesy of the Weyauwega Public Library.)

HARDEN HOUSE AT 107 EAST PARKER STREET. Attorney John Fordyce, who resided here with his family from about 1863 to 1911, built this home on East Parker Street. In 1911, businessman Fred Harden, shown in the foreground with wife, Nora, and their daughters, purchased the property. (Courtesy of the Weyauwega Public Library.)

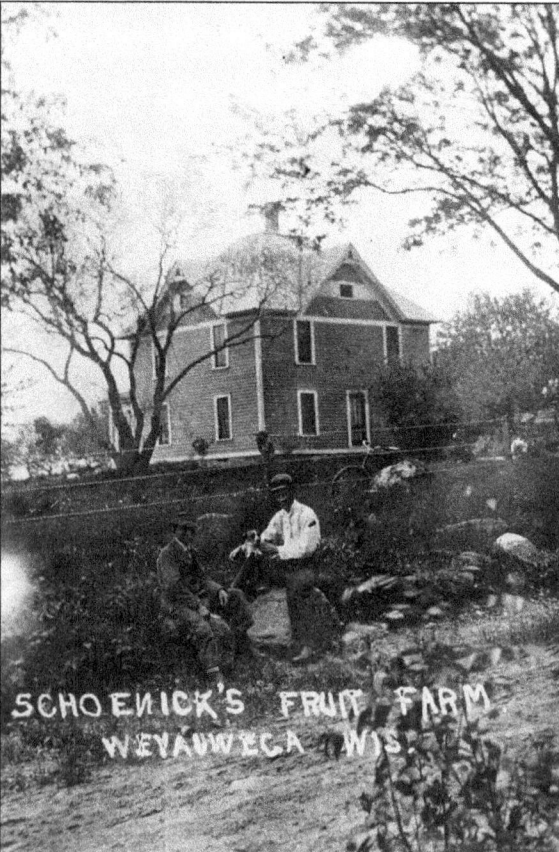

SCHOENICK FARM. This is the farm of William Schoenick. After the brewery partnership was dissolved, Schoenick became a butcher and purchased a farm. (Courtesy of Florence Oehlke.)

Seven

DOWNTOWN

A RAINY DAY, 1901. Cement sidewalks were installed in 1901 at the insistence of A.L. Hutchinson, village president. Here, a man strolls in the rain on the new sidewalks. The first electric light system was installed in 1894. It would be hard to imagine all the shops and grocery stores surrounded by large, three-story homes with a park during the prime of Weyauwega. It was a working community that worked for its residents. (Courtesy of the Weyauwega Public Library.)

EAST MAIN STREET WITH ANDREW WATTERSTON STORE, C. 1896. Andrew Watterston, a native of Scotland, operated a store on the southeast corner of Mill and Main Streets in the 1890s. He handled general merchandise, clothing, dry goods, footwear, and staple and fancy groceries. His sons William and James worked in his business. (Courtesy of the Weyauwega Public Library.)

WIENER BROTHERS' BOSTON STORE. Ben and Ike Wiener leased this building in 1903 and bought it in 1908 for their Boston Store. This is the same store as above. They were in business for 30 years. This was probably the busiest corner on Main Street with the hotel, Exchange Building, and bank on the other corners. (Courtesy of Florence Oehlke.)

EAST MAIN STREET FROM HOTEL. Stores on the Pioneer Block were, from left to right, the Weed, Gumaer & Co. bank, Andrew Gardner's hardware, and W.A. Weisbrod Dry Goods and Grocery. The Catholic church can be seen in the background. (Courtesy of the Weyauwega Public Library.)

VAN EPPS STORE. Peter Van Epps owned a produce and moving business on North Mill Street. This was the site that later became Tony Kirsling's blacksmith shop. Van Epps was involved in building the road from Gills Landing to Weyauwega. He was active in the Grand Army of the Republic and Legion posts in town. He was a Civil War soldier. This photograph is pre-1902. (Courtesy of the Weyauwega Public Library.)

Main Street West of Mill Street. Looking west on Mill Street, Anklam's Hall is the prominent building with the false front, which was originally put up by Henry Stier. To the right are the harness shop of David Wafler and a meat market. Lakeside Creamery with the taller smokestacks was behind Main Street. (Courtesy of the Weyauwega Public Library.)

Wagon Downtown. This is a great photograph of the busiest corner with the Hutchinson Hotel in the middle and the Watterston Store. The building behind the wagon had burned down, and a newer one was built in its place. There were a total of three different buildings at that location. (Courtesy of Florence Oehlke.)

JOHN J.L. ROHDES ON MAIN STREET. This is how Main Street looked as John J.L. Rohdes walked the boardwalk in 1897. Rohdes was born on October 20, 1831, in Germany, and died on September 4, 1911. His headstone reads that he was in the 5th US Army as a sergeant in Company A. He is buried in Oakwood Cemetery. The boy on the bike was William Wafler, son of David Wafler. (Courtesy of the Weyauwega Public Library.)

MAIN STREET LOOKING WEST. With Anklam's Hall on the left and the Masonic lodge on the right, this is how Main Street looked facing east. This postcard does not have a date, but the image was taken before concrete sidewalks were installed. Herman Anklam Sr. was born in Germany on November 9, 1853, and died on May 3, 1919. (Courtesy of the Weyauwega Public Library.)

STREET SCENE LOOKING WEST. This view was taken right after the sidewalks were poured. The tall building on the right was the First National Bank. A tobacco shop was a couple of doors away. The Exchange Building is shown with its spire across the street. A barbershop was on the left, with the village hall located in the middle of the stores. (Courtesy of the Weyauwega Public Library.)

POTTER STORE AND WILCOX STORE. H.W. Potter and Company on Main Street, with its large awning, would be hard to miss. The store sold dry goods and general merchandise. Potter and Company was established in 1868 in a 50-by-80-foot building. Potter advertised a prime set of mink furs for $15. He was a member Knights of Phythias. W.W. Crane purchased the store in 1884. The Wilcox Store was on the right. Chris Nelson got his start in this store. (Courtesy of the Weyauwega Public Library.)

VILLAGE HALL. In 1915, the village hall was erected at a cost of over $10,000. With the fire department on the street level, the fire apparatus, which was capable of throwing three streams over the highest buildings in town, occupied the first-floor front. In the rear was the village jail. The upper floor contained the public library in front and a council room and auditorium in the rear. (Courtesy of the Weyauwega Public Library.)

FIRE DEPARTMENT. The first fire with impact to the community was in 1857; it destroyed the Matthews Boot and Shoe store. Over the years, the Weyauwegian Building, the post office, the Weed, Gumaer & Co. bank, and the Mills Grocery store were also taken out by fire. Fire equipment was feeble at best in the early days. Early firefighters grabbed available horses off Main Street in the event of a fire, and owners were paid for their use. (Courtesy of the Weyauwega Public Library.)

BOSTON STORE, IGA STORE, AND MERCHANTS BANK. The Boston Store on the right was owned and operated by Ben Wiener and his brother Ike for 35 years. They were born in Russia around 1850. William Weed provided the backing they needed to rent space on Main Street. It was destroyed by fire in 1933 and rebuilt in 1934. Ike died in 1935, and Ben continued to operate the business until 1939. He died in 1952. (Courtesy of Florence Oehlke.)

MASONIC LODGE NO. 82. Seven Masons organized the Free and Accepted Masonic Lodge No. 82 on West Main Street in 1856. It was formally chartered in 1857 as the first Masonic lodge in Waupaca County. Its three principal officers were Louis Bostedo, Elias Bates, and William Gumaer. The lodge building was erected and dedicated in 1888. Prior to that, the lodge met in various locations. (Courtesy of the Weyauwega Public Library.)

Eight

VILLAGE LIFE

GEORGE HAIRE DANCING. George Haire (right) is shown dancing with Henry Myers at a masquerade party. Dancing was popular at Whitney Hall and other venues. There will be a broad portrait of life in Weyauwega presented in this chapter. There was everything from road building to people having fun with music, plays, parades, organizations, and the fair. Sometimes it is hard to believe that this was the wilderness. (Courtesy of the Weyauwega Public Library.)

GIANT ONION POSTCARD. While this is a spoof postcard, Peter L. Van Epps did grow a 157-pound, 12-ounce pumpkin in 1890. He used R. Shumway seeds for the pumpkin. He also received the best Jersey cow and best heifer cow awards in October 1889 at the Waupaca County Fair. (Courtesy of Florence Oehlke.)

GREETING CARD. This is a postcard from the 1920s. Several styles of postcards have been found. Some were doctored but all of them promoted Weyauwega. Fishing was always popular in the area, with some of the best water in the state available only miles away, and some postcards reflected that interest. (Courtesy of Florence Oehlke.)

MUSIC SHOW ON FEBRUARY 28, 1912. Amateur musical entertainments by townspeople were typical of the time. This photograph was taken on February 28, 1912. From left to right are Susie Bennett, Winnie Bennett Peterson, Florence Baldwin, and George Farley, with Mrs. May Bennett standing. (Courtesy of the Weyauwega Public Library.)

WINIFRED BENNETT PETERSON MANUSCRIPT. Winifred Bennett Peterson, born in 1883, spent most of her 100-plus years in Weyauwega. She graduated from Weyauwega High School in 1901, Downer College in Milwaukee, and then studied music at the University of Wisconsin at Madison. She played piano for silent movies in Weyauwega and at neighboring Waupaca. She gave private piano and vocal lessons and toured with the Lyceum Company of Chicago as a singer and accompanist. (Courtesy of the Weyauwega Public Library.)

"My Old Hometown-Weyauwega"
Dedicated to E.A. Agard - Fairbury, Ill - Nov. 16, 1935

Winifred Bennett Peterson 1883-1984
Arr. By Jon M. Peterson

Copyright 2005
Jon M. Peterson

JULY 4, 1897, PARADE. In this 1897 photograph, the band plays as the parade travels east from the Exchange Building on the Fourth of July. In July 1882, 2,000 people attended the Fourth of July celebration. The streets were decorated with evergreens and flags. The parade featured a band and glee club. Exercises were held at the square, the afternoon had races on Main Street, and fireworks were set off near the school. (Courtesy of the Weyauwega Public Library.)

ROYAL NEIGHBORS, JULY 4, 1908. In the July 4, 1908, parade, a pony pulled the Royal Neighbors' float. Shown from left to right are Mrs. John Frederick, Mrs. A. Cizinsky, Mrs. Wm. Haire, Mrs. Otto Greir, Mrs. Jay Doney, Mrs. B. Bellinger, Mrs. Leo Walrath, Mrs. Charles Ter Haar, Mrs. A.J. Rieck, Mrs. Fred Hertz, Mrs. H.J. Becker, and driver John Doney. The Royal Neighbors was a Fraternal Insurance Company. (Courtesy of the Weyauwega Public Library.)

JULY 4, 1911. Dressed for the July 4, 1911, celebration are, from left to right: (first row) N. Peterson, ? Pope, L. Weise, Anita Roloff Romon, and Agnes Andrews; (second row) Gladys Lawrence, S. Schoenick, L. Mitchell, L. Lawrence, Harriette Rice, and Viola Peterson; (third row) Pearl Hazen, Mary Uttormark, Merna Bork Frost, Irene Wolfram, Edna George, and Ella Andrews. (Courtesy of the Weyauwega Public Library.)

JULY 4, 1919, PARADE. On this 1919 Fourth of July pony-drawn float are, from left to right, Bernice Lilly, Nolan Olson, Kenneth Peterson, Laura Rohde, Ruth Wiesbrod, and Earl Kellet. The Fourth of July parades were always popular. In 1890, the Fourth of July program included an industrial parade led by the cornet band, exhibits, balloon ascensions, and fireworks. (Courtesy of the Weyauwega Public Library.)

RED CROSS IN PARADE. This parade was typical of the World War I period with the Honor Squad leading with the American flag, followed by the Red Cross. (Courtesy of the Weyauwega Public Library.)

ROAD WORK. The road to Weyauwega from nearby Fremont was a seven-mile corduroy road. Local men were hired to run slushers (levelers), wheel scrapers, and graders. Four horse teams pulled equipment. The road, US Highway 10, became part of the "Yellowstone Trail" and was concreted by 1927. A large concrete mixer moved along as smaller train cars, filled with dry concrete mix, were delivered to the site. (Courtesy of the Weyauwega Public Library.)

MAKING ROADS. Dirt is being carried away in order to make a road in the area. Seems like hard labor, as roads were dug and wagons were loaded by hand. Horses were the backbone of that labor. The highway to Weyauwega was a big deal. It changed routes from water travel to over-the-road. (Courtesy of the Weyauwega Public Library.)

GRAVEL QUARRY. It is sometimes hard to remember the backbreaking work that took place in order to get roads in the country. Horse-drawn wagons traveled miles to carry debris away and to haul gravel back to the job site. Quarry pits were dug, and rocks and stones were turned to gravel, which was then loaded onto wagons. Limestone is prevalent in the area and makes great gravel. (Courtesy of the Weyauwega Public Library.)

GOOD TEMPLARS. According to the *Weyauwega Astonisher* on October 9, 1888, "The Good Templars was the largest temperance organization in existence. Its rituals were translated into fourteen different languages on every continent on the globe." Pictured are, from left to right, (first row) Harry Bennett, Pliny Myers, Gus Meyers, and George Meyers; (second row) Frances Cates, Ida Regan Rich, Agnes Bennett, Nettie Ritchie, Ida Keeney, and Alice Bennett. (Courtesy of the Weyauwega Public Library.)

MODERN WOODSMEN UNION CAMP 1232. In no specific order are the following identified men: (first row) James Mathwig, James Vincent, L.C. Loss, H.J. Becker, Gus Bork, B.H. Denninger, and Henry Waterhouse; (second row) E. Brown, G. Scheel, and George Stafford; (third row) George Haire. The photograph was taken in front of the Woods Hotel on July 4, 1884. (Courtesy of the Weyauwega Public Library.)

LATE 1880s VILLAGE BAND. The village band played at the bandstand at the square and at Whitney Hall. Members are, from left to right, (first row) Herb Keeney, Ollie Pike, Harv Rowe, Bill Bubitz, Will Wafler, Charles Goodnow, and John McCall; (second row) Bern Bellinger, Bert Wells, Willis Caley, Cas. Kulibert, Chris Olson, L. Clark, and Dave Watterson. (Courtesy of the Weyauwega Public Library.)

BOY SCOUTS, AUGUST 1919. The Boy Scouts in August 1919 are, from left to right, (first row) Clyde Keeney, Albert Wiese, ? Paap, Roscoe Miller, Mel Smith, Claude Peterson, Reed Dunbar, George Williams, and Dr. Popelars, the scoutmaster; (second row) Mel Romon, Eugene Behnke, William Murton, Chris Olson, Arden Joerns, ? McCue, Tom Gerlach, and Frank McIntyre. Standing alone is Albert Weisbrod. Dr. Popelars was a veterinarian. (Courtesy of the Weyauwega Public Library.)

Spoof Photograph, 1913. In a 1913 spoof postcard, Weyauwega has a high-rise building. Spoof postcards were common during that time. (Courtesy of the Weyauwega Public Library.)

Fire Trucks of Weyauwega. Firemen are assembled here with two of the older fire trucks of Weyauwega. The first fire engine that arrived in Weyauwega in 1889 was named *Weyauwega No. 1.* The fire of 1857 took out several businesses at a loss of $5,000—a lot of money in those days. The fire department was organized in 1885. (Courtesy of the Weyauwega Public Library.)

Waupaca County Fair. Women in their stylish hats and men in their suits wander around the fairgrounds going from tent to tent. Horse shows and races were as popular then as they are today. Vendors showed their wares, and others sold goods in the agricultural market. (Courtesy of the Weyauwega Public Library.)

Fairgrounds. Buildings were erected on the fairgrounds to show that it was going to be a permanent event. Note the Harley Davidson leaning against the tree and the Model T parked near the building. This building remains on the grounds today. (Courtesy of the Weyauwega Public Library.)

SURREY RACING AT THE FAIRGROUNDS, C. 1906. Surrey racing was a popular sport in Waupaca County and at the county fairgrounds in Weyauwega. People raised horses just for surrey racing and took great pride in them. Dr. Corbett, a Mason and a member of the Modern Woodsmen, loved fine horses, and one in particular named Flash Mills. (Courtesy of the Weyauwega Public Library.)

COUNTY FAIR. Young and old are shown waiting for the next surrey race at the fair. The first county fair in Weyauwega was held at Turner Gardens on the east side of town. In 1872, the fair association bought four acres for $60. In 1875, the association purchased a field of 16 acres from January Carpenter. The first fair there was October 15 and 16, 1875. (Courtesy of the Weyauwega Public Library.)

PHOTOGRAPHER AT THE FAIR, 1883. In the foreground, a photographer takes a picture of two young women while others mill about the grounds with the bandstand at center rear. Considering Weyauwega is not the county seat, the fair is a busy time for the area. Henry House is the man to the right of the photographer. Again, the ladies are wearing the latest in hat wear. (Courtesy of Carol Toepke.)

Visit us at
arcadiapublishing.com

www.ingramcontent.com/pod-product-compliance
Lightning Source LLC
Chambersburg PA
CBHW050611110426
42813CB00008B/2524